CRITICAL STUDIES OF
KEY TEXTS

James Joyce's
Ulysses

D1420243

Other titles available in the series

Liz Bellamy
Jonathan Swift's Gulliver's Travels

Nicola Bradbury
Charles Dickens' Great Expectations

David Fuller
James Joyce's Ulysses

Pauline Nestor
Charlotte Bronte's Jane Eyre

Suzanne Raitt
Virginia Woolf's To the Lighthouse

Gene Ruoff
Jane Austen's Sense and Sensibility

David Seed
James Joyce's A Portrait of the Artist as a Young Man

T. R. Wright
George Eliot's Middlemarch

James Joyce's
Ulysses

David Fuller

University of Durham

HARVESTER
WHEATSHEAF

New York   London   Toronto   Sydney   Tokyo   Singapore

First published 1992 by
Harvester Wheatsheaf,
66 Wood Lane End, Hemel Hempstead
Hertfordshire, HP2 4RG

A division of
Simon & Schuster International Group

Typeset in 10½ on 12pt Sabon by
STM Typesetting Ltd., Amesbury, Wilts.

Printed and bound in Great Britian by
Billing and Sons Ltd, Worcester

British Library Cataloguing in Publication Data

Fuller, David
James Joyce's "Ulysses".
I. Title
823

ISBN 0-7450-0573-X
ISBN 0-7450-0574-8 pbk ✓

1   2   3   4   5   95   94   93   92

Contents

Note on the Text

There can be no definitive text of *Ulysses*. The main substantive texts are the first edition of 1922, the Random House edition of 1961 (which replaced, with corrections, the first American edition of 1934), and the corrected text of 1984, 1986 (see Bibliography). The corrected text, though still widely regarded as standard, has been attacked on various grounds: amongst others, that it adopts readings from sources not in a direct line of descent to Joyce's final text of 1922; that it at times prefers readings derived from evidence of Joyce's first thoughts, despite a strong case for later versions; that it corrects, not from Joyce's manuscripts, but from facsimiles which do not reproduce the originals adequately for its purposes; that it normalises errors and inconsistencies which are clearly Joyce's; and that it does not retain typographical features of 1922 which Joyce apparently approved. The edition has therefore generated considerable scholarly controversy. This can be followed up in C. George Sandulescu and Clive Hart (eds), *Assessing the 1984 'Ulysses'*, Princess Grace Irish Library, 1, Gerrards Cross, Colin Smythe, 1986; polemically, in John Kidd, 'The Scandal of *Ulysses*', *New York Review of Books*, XXXV, 11 (30 June 1988), 32–9; in detail in John Kidd, 'An Inquiry into *Ulysses: The Corrected Text*', *Papers of the Bibliographical Society of America*, 82, 4 (1988), 411–584. The substantive texts can be checked for principal variants against Philip Gaskell and Clive Hart, *'Ulysses': A review of three texts*, Princess Grace Irish Library, 4, Gerrards Cross, Colin Smythe, 1989.

Note on the Text

In the following study, quotations are from 1986. References are to 1986 and 1961 respectively. Short quotations are not referenced where their approximate location is sufficiently obvious from the surrounding discussion. Where it seemed necessary a line reference is given to the lineated version of 1986 (the 'Student's Edition'), thus 448,3353/549 means 1986, page 448, episode line 3353; 1961, page 549.

CITATIONS AND ABBREVIATIONS

The following abbreviations have been used for titles of works by Joyce.

CW	Critical Writings
D	Dubliners
E	Exiles
FW	Finnegans Wake
P	A Portrait of the Artist as a Young Man
SH	Stephen Hero
SL	Selected Letters
U	Ulysses

JJ   This refers to the biography of Joyce by Richard Ellman

The bibliography should be consulted for full details.

Acknowledgements

It is a pleasure to acknowledge the help of friends and colleagues who have read, commented on, or otherwise helped with parts of this book. Tom Craik, David Crane, Cynthia Fuller, Ben Knights, Michael O'Neill, Gareth Reeves, Michael Schepers, Derek Todd, Patricia Waugh and George J. B. Watson gave assistance generously, as did a group of staff, students and friends of Durham University who over a six-month period took part in a reading of *Finnegans Wake* leading up to the fiftieth anniversary of its publication. Agnes Delanoy skilfully and with unfailing good humour converted convoluted manuscript into clean typescript.

I am grateful to the James Joyce Foundation, Zürich, and to its director, Fritz Senn, for the opportunity to talk through a part of the book, and to Durham University for a period of research leave in which to complete it.

Preface

Joyce's lectures and essays, his letters and his conversations as recorded by Arthur Power and the many friends and associates interviewed by Richard Ellmann, like the books on *Ulysses* by Stuart Gilbert and Frank Budgen which he sponsored, all show that he endorsed some central traditional interests of criticism: interests in character, in theme, and in the construction of a fully imagined social world. It is indicative of Joyce's predispositions that Tolstoy was among his favourite novelists. Joyce's radically experimental attitudes to form, language and the presentation of consciousness have also generated, and become the subject of experimental critiques with roots in anthropology, linguistics and psychoanalysis, some underlying bases of which are described below (pp. 24–8). This study works with both the critical methods Joyce endorsed and those his work has played a major part in generating. Opposed to the Catholic appropriation of Joyce which does not acknowledge that his lifelong dialogue with the Church was an antagonistic one, and to the post-structuralist appropriation of his work as concerned exclusively with language, this study stresses the political dimension of Joyce's fiction – his socialism, his attitude to Irish nationalism, his prescient treatment of racism and anti-Semitism, and the relation of these issues to the mode of *Ulysses*, comedy, which Joyce saw as ethical and political, a force against fanaticism. I have also discussed Joyce's radical experimentation with form and language, and his challenges to notions of the individual subject and to stereotypes of male sexual identity. Many of these issues are dealt with whilst following the episodic structure within which the novel gives rise to them, partly because more synoptic criticism does not always lead back readily into the novel, and partly because it can lose touch with some basic pleasures of reading Joyce: the radiant clarity of his precise observations of world and mind, and his immense inventiveness with words.

Ulysses stands alone. Like any individual work, however, it can in some ways be seen more clearly by comparison within its author's whole *oeuvre*. I have referred, therefore, as necessary to *Dubliners* and later work to extend the account of Joyce's portrayal of Ireland and Catholicism, to *Exiles* and its treatment of sexuality, to *A Portrait of the Artist as a Young Man* and *Stephen Hero* from which the character of Stephen Dedalus is in part taken, and to *Finnegans Wake*, where the character and myth of HCE extends aspects of Odysseus–Bloom, and in which Joyce's pressure on the limits of English, and his love of the music of language, are so evident.

My own interests in critical theory and practice lie in acknowledging and working with the inevitably personal nature of criticism, and in encouraging an interplay of practice and theory, such that each can question, and as necessary disrupt, the other. In discussing literature, personal response is vital because a text achieves significant life in the mind of a reader. What we understand a text to mean, because that text is addressing in each of us a particular complex of thought and feeling, is bound to be involved with the experience we bring to it. Why this should be so is clear if we consider how interpretation works. As we read, we notice aspects of a text which connect with our own experience alongside others highlighted by kinds of stress – of position, repetition, intensity of articulation, and so on – given by the author. We also, in ways suggested by Henry James's metaphor of the figure in the carpet, establish relationships between all the highlighted elements. Personal perspectives are inevitably and properly active both in responding to particulars and in the pattern-making from which overall meanings emerge. If criticism is to represent all that happens in the reading process, it must incorporate the values and experiences with which a text interacts. To do this is to encourage reading which calls on all the faculties that must be brought into activity – intellect, feeling, imagination – in any proper knowledge of art. If we accept that the personal is not purely individual – either that it bears more or less fully the traces of our own cultural situation, or that there is a core of common experience which a personal view that goes deep enough will tap – this view of criticism will not mean generating purely private meanings. But there must also be completion by a pressure to go beyond the personal – recognising that one never entirely can. One reason for acknowledging the personal nature of interpretation and evaluation is to make criticism more real. Another, quite different in direction, is to acquire some control over unconscious subjective distortion. One point of writing criticism is to engage with the frames of reference of one's own culture, and to re-engage older texts with the forms of intellect and sensibility generated by new conditions. But one point of reading imaginative literature at all is to get outside our own cultural presuppositions and experience surrogately alternative views of the world. Criticism locks us into our own cultural situation if it does not attempt – acknowledging all the difficulties of this – to see 'the object as in itself it really is'. Criticism may help investigate and deepen our own intellectual, emotional and imaginative set. It should not simply confirm it. Art is not to be enlisted as propaganda for one's own view of the world. Overtly personal criticism can avoid being narrowly subjective by taking into account all those elements in interpretation which can act as controls on the solipsistic. We should always be able to believe that the author's best self could recognise a reading as legitimate, that a reading has taken account of the meanings a text could have for its first audience, and the changing meanings a text has had for later readers who bring to it different presuppositions. Personal response is always central. However deeply investigated, it is never all. In the attempt to make a text fully and truly a part of ourselves we must, if we are to extend that self, move outside it. We can never completely do so.

Preface

Interpretation avowedly involved with non-literary experience inevitably calls on ethical, political or religious perspectives. This does not imply a separation of literary and non-literary values: readers naturally derive their values in part from the records of human imaginative experience. It does mean acknowledging that any reading is interacting with a set of values, values which it may change. And it means saying where a reading stands in relation to those values. There should be a similar interplay between individual readings and general theories of reading. Theories of reading are properly derived from all one has read, with practice and theory negotiating a constant interaction. The conscious application of theory can be part of an attempt to understand one's own conditioning and to evolve a principled critique of it with the aim of making one's own alternatives to the world as one finds it consistent and coherent, not just intellectually but in one's whole mode of acting and being. Theory can help to free people from the effect of destructive ideologies. But it can also be yet another destructive net or trap. The form of this currently most evident in academic criticism is the barren intellectualism which enjoys the prestige of an imposing language and the safety of a pretended objectivity while pursuing a career the dynamics of which create a need for new fashions. There are also less conditional problems: of subscribing to a hierarchy in which abstract intellectual consciousness is seen as superior to other forms of knowledge; of accepting in the humanities criteria of knowledge governed by those of the economically more powerful natural sciences; of getting control by means of a narrow but powerful form of intellectual operation over art that should properly be intellectually and emotionally disruptive; of operating a closed circuit of rigid method in which answers are entirely predicted by questions. Roland Barthes has a fine phrase, applicable here, on 'the sclerosis of systems'. One characteristic of imaginative literature is its particularity, which should always resist the generalising tendency of system. If a theory does not allow this resistance to break down its schemes it becomes merely self-confirming, seeing only what it sets out to find. The myth critic finds a pattern very like a seasonal cycle. The deconstructive critic finds criticism participating in a text's endless play of meanings. And so on. Properly, the individual text must be allowed to 'read' the theories applied to it: that is, to resist and reshape them. This can only happen if we allow a text, in the first instance, to generate the terms in which it is read. The basis for this is not the chimera of unconditioned intuition: we can never make sense of anything without a framework within which to do so. But neither is it true, as evangelists of theory are wont to claim, that only theoretically self-conscious criticism is not in the grip of some given theory. Learned frameworks of critical response are always subject to the powerful check of the actual experience of a text struggling to be true to itself in articulation. There are more ways out of mental prisons than the hardly guaranteed exit, all too appealing to intellectuals, of yet more self-consciousness. The proper basis for a desirably resistant, disruptive engagement with general theories of reading is that of having struggled to make the fullest possible sense of many different kinds of writing in many different kinds of ways.[1]

I

Contexts

Historical and Cultural Context

Ulysses was written, as its final page says, in Trieste, Zürich, and Paris between 1914 and 1921 – that is, it was begun in the Austro–Hungarian Empire at the beginning of the Great War, continued through the war in neutral Switzerland, and finished in the centre of post-war avant-garde. When Joyce began the novel he had published only essays and reviews and the slim volume of poems, *Chamber Music* (1907). *A Portrait of the Artist as a Young Man* began serial publication in *The Egoist* in February 1914, and after many struggles the collection of stories, *Dubliners* (completed in 1907), finally appeared in June the same year. Joyce embarked on one of the greatest experiments in modern literature while still a virtually unknown writer, though the publication of *A Portrait* in book form (1916), and of sections of *Ulysses* itself in *The Little Review* from 1918, were to bring him celebrity as the work progressed. In Ireland the period during which Joyce worked on *Ulysses* is the time of the 1916 Easter Rising against British rule, effective secession after the general election of 1918, the Anglo–Irish war of 1919-21, the creation of the new state of Northern Ireland in 1921, and, in January 1922, the setting up of the Irish Free State. Joyce never returned to Ireland after a brief visit of 1912 connected with the possible publication of *Dubliners*. He expressed little interest in events in Ireland from the Easter Rising to the setting up of the Free State. On the Great War he took a neutralist attitude: 'Dooleysprudence' (CW, 246–8) (1916) criticises the moral propaganda of both sides. The principal historical context of *Ulysses* is not the period of its composition but the period of its setting, 1904.

In relation to *Ulysses* this context is best understood as far as possible from Joyce's own writings: fiction, essays and letters. The central figure is Charles Stewart Parnell (1846–91), and the main issue Irish independence of Britain. Parnell and the Home Rule movements had roots, going back at least to the eighteenth century, in events to which Joyce often refers, or of which he presumes a knowledge. Only occasionally in *Ulysses* does Joyce refer back substantially beyond the eighteenth century to a crucial origin of Anglo–Irish conflict, the Norman invasion of Ireland in the twelfth century at the invitation of Dermot MacMurrough, King of Leinster. This beginning of the English conquest of Ireland, supposedly legitimised by a papal bull, *Laudabiliter*, issued by the only English pope, Nicholas Breakspear, Pope Adrian IV, contained in Joyce's view the main elements of the subsequent history: English tyranny and Irish betrayal, by Ireland itself and by the Catholic Church. It is a view which Joyce set out in plain terms in his fullest statement on Anglo–Irish history, 'Ireland, Land of Saints and Sages' (1907) (CW, 153–74). In *Ulysses* (and even in *Finnegans Wake* where earlier Irish history is much more fully invoked) Joyce largely ignores Tudor, Stuart and Cromwellian policy towards Ireland, the phase of history leading up to William of Orange's victory at the Battle of the Boyne in 1690. The historical background of *Ulysses* after Henry II means principally the 1798 republican risings, the Act of Union of 1800, and the various parliamentary, popular and insurrectionary movements of the nineteenth century. The risings of 1798 (there were a number, more or less co-ordinated throughout the country) grew out of the Society of United Irishmen founded in 1791 by Wolfe Tone (1763–98) and others. The aim of the risings, which were preceded by brutal British army and Irish Orange lodge (Protestant) repression of the Society, was to found a secular republic on the model of (and helped by) the new republic of revolutionary France. They were put down quickly and with great ferocity. The fear in ruling-class circles which this evidence of widespread disaffection generated led to the Act of Union – 'the transaction of buying and selling the Dublin parliament', as Joyce called it (CW, 223). By this Act the Dublin parliament dissolved itself and transferred its powers to the British parliament. The other aftermath of '98 was the rising of 1803 led by Robert Emmet (1778–1803). This was easily crushed, and Emmet was executed, but his speech from the dock became part of Irish historical mythology. (Joyce, not one to endorse models of Romantic failure in history or in myth, thought Emmet's rising foolish (CW, 189); in *Ulysses* Bloom farts through his recollection of the famous speech (238–9/291), and Emmet's death may, as Richard Ellmann suggests (CW, 189), be the basis for the grotesque Cyclops parody of the execution of a nationalist hero (U, 251–5/306–10).

The Act of Union led to over a century of agitation for the restoration of Home Rule, the first important figure in which is Daniel O'Connell, 'The Liberator' (1775–1847). O'Connell's main aim, apart from repeal of the Union, was Catholic emancipation, meaning equal political and civil rights for Catholics. Barred from parliament until emancipation in 1829, O'Connell developed various methods of extra-parliamentary agitation, particularly bringing pressure to bear on government by shows of popular support at huge public meetings. O'Connell's policy was non-violent, where possible was constitutional, and allied nationalism with the Catholic Church. Though he achieved Catholic emancipation his efforts for repeal of the Union failed, and political activity was in any case driven into new channels by the terrible famines in Ireland caused by potato blight from 1845 to 1848. In the early 1840s a new movement, Young Ireland, began under O'Connell, but its ideals had more in common than O'Connell's had with the revolutionary generation of '98. Its members were not at one with O'Connell in his association with the Catholic Church or his opposition to the use of force. Provoked by the extreme situation of the famines, they split from O'Connell's Repeal

Association under the leadership of Smith O'Brien (1803–64). Nothing effective was done against the famines. O'Connell died in 1847. Neither party recovered from the split. The famines caused the deaths and emigration (mostly to America) of over a million people between 1845 and 1848 alone, as well as continued massive emigration during the following two decades. Overall the population of Ireland declined from eight million in the census of 1841 to four and a half million in that of 1901, giving some justification to the arguments of the violent nationalist of *Ulysses* (Cyclops). Though the immediate cause of the famines, the potato blight, was an act of God or of Nature, the ultimate causes were political: British failure to deal with long-recognised problems of the Irish economy, problems which were arguably – and this was how Joyce himself saw them (*CW*, 167, 199) – actively created by British policy.

The English politician to attempt most in Ireland in the nineteenth century was the Liberal Prime Minister, William Ewart Gladstone (1809–98). Gladstone began his first ministry in 1868 in the immediate aftermath of another revolutionary attempt to overthrow British government of Ireland: the revolt organised in 1867 by the Fenian movement led by James Stephens (1824–1901). Gladstone's first step (1869) was to disestablish the (Protestant) Church of Ireland, which meant that Irish Catholics were no longer forced to support it with tithes. Land reform then became a principal issue. It was promoted by the Land League founded in 1879 by Michael Davitt (1846–1906) to protect tenant farmers against exorbitant rents and eviction. The movement worked hand-in-hand with a renewed struggle for Home Rule in which the principal figure was Parnell. Gladstone's first Home Rule Bill of 1886 foundered on the opposition of the Ulster Protestants, to whom it signified 'Rome Rule'. There followed an attempt to discredit Parnell by a forger, Richard Piggott (Joyce made great play with the Piggott forgeries in *Finnegans Wake*), which was itself based on a piece of political violence several times referred to in *Ulysses*: the murder in 1882 of the Chief Secretary and the Undersecretary for Ireland in Phoenix Park, Dublin, by a group calling itself the Invincibles.

In 1887 Piggott, an Irish journalist, published letters which implicated Parnell in the planning of these murders. The letters were exposed as forgeries and Parnell was vindicated. But in 1889 Parnell's position was undermined in more serious terms by what were for Joyce the most formative events of contemporary Irish politics. Parnell was cited in a divorce suit brought on grounds of adultery by Captain William O'Shea. Parnell's relationship with Mrs O'Shea began in 1880. It was both clandestine and well known. But when, as a result of the divorce scandal, Gladstone decided that the Liberals could not work with the Irish Parliamentary Party so long as Parnell remained its leader. Parnell was ousted by a revolt from within his own party led by Timothy Healy and was subsequently denounced by the Catholic Church. He died in 1891.

The place and importance of Parnell in Joyce's family background and in Irish life generally is evident in *A Portrait of the Artist* in the passionate argument over Christmas dinner, 1891, about the role of the Church in Parnell's fall. By 1902, in the *Dubliners* story 'Ivy Day in the Committee Room', Parnell has become part of a past of heroic myth in an utterly different key from the trivia of contemporary politics. That Joyce's father passed on to Joyce his own admiration of Parnell can be supposed from Joyce's lost childhood poem, 'Et tu, Healy', written at the time of Parnell's death when Joyce was nine. It is clear from the title that the poem compared Parnell's associate, Timothy Healy, to Brutus as the friend and betrayer of Julius Caesar. For Joyce this became an archetypal Irish situation: betrayal – national and personal – is one of his recurrent subjects. Parnell is a central figure for Joyce's imagination because his downfall – as Joyce saw it, betrayal by associates completed by the denunciation of the Church – epitomised for Joyce so much about Irish life, politics and religion. In 'Gas from a Burner' (1912) Joyce compared his own treatment over the publication of *Dubliners* with the brutality of the Irish to Parnell after his fall, while in *Finnegans Wake* Joyce is Parnell in another way: Parnell's 'No man has a right to fix the boundary of the march of a nation' is adapted to act as one justification of Joyce's experiments with language (*FW*, 292). In 'The Shade of Parnell', an essay on the eventual passing of a Home Rule Bill for Ireland in 1912, Joyce used of Parnell the imagery he gives to the visionary nationalist John F. Taylor in *Ulysses* (116–17/142–3): Parnell is the Moses who led his people from the Egyptian bondage of English tyranny to the verge of the Promised Land of Independence. At the end of the essay he becomes Christ betrayed by Judas. It is Caesar and Brutus of the childhood poem, but in a higher key, and indicates amply the central and symbolic position of Parnell in Joyce's imagination of Ireland.

The replacement of Parnell in the Irish Parliamentary Party helped Ireland not at all: Gladstone's second Home Rule Bill was defeated in 1892. The Gaelic League was founded in 1893 to further Irish culture and particularly the Irish language, which both Joyce and Stephen briefly attempted to learn (*JJ*, 61; *SH*, 58; *P*, 206). The early motto of the League was 'Sinn Féin' – 'We Ourselves', or 'Ourselves Alone'. 'Sinn Féin' was therefore well in the air by 1904 – Bloom mixes with what Molly, not perfectly familiar with the slogan, calls 'those Sinner Fein' – though in the interests of a comprehensive politics Joyce may antedate a little. Sinn Féin was first established as a distinct political organisation in the following year by Arthur Griffith (1872–1922), first Prime Minister of the Irish Free State, and the last important figure of Irish politics to appear in *Ulysses*.

This is the nightmare history from which Stephen is trying to awake, and which threatens to engulf him; one of the nets flung out, in *A Portrait of the Artist*, to trap the would-be free individual. These are the nationalist movements, from the Land League to Sinn Féin, in which Bloom takes an active interest.

When, writing to Edmund Gosse in Gosse's capacity as an official of the Royal Literary Fund, Yeats described Joyce as a man who 'disliked politics' (*Letters*, II, 362), it seems clear that Yeats combined scrupulous honesty in phrasing his remarks with saying what was necessary during the Great War to get Joyce money from the fund. In fact, at certain times in his life Joyce showed great interest in politics: socialist, anarchist and nationalist, theoretical and practical.[1] Joyce was probably in the position he describes as Stephen's – an ally of collectivist politics not because he felt direct transformation of society his own mission, but because he was so fundamentally opposed to aspects of society as he found it (*SH*, 133). Socialism was, for Joyce, an ally against the religious and social tyrannies which he so fervently rejected.[2] He first attended meetings of socialist groups immediately before he went to France in 1902.[3] By 1904 he identified himself as a socialist, and a 'socialistic artist' (*Letters*, II, 68, 89), not making any special point about conversion but rather on the assumption that this was axiomatic. While in Trieste he followed closely the debates within the Italian Socialist Congress of 1906. With a note of triumph unusual in Joyce the peroration of the essay, 'A Portrait of the Artist' (1904), predicts the victory of 'the generous idea', socialism, born inevitably from 'the competitive order'[4]: the violence of capitalism is self-defeating. Joyce's active interest in socialism during the years in which *Dubliners* was written lessened after 1907, though a letter of that year which remarks that his socialism has left him need not be taken too seriously: it goes on immediately to say he has lost interest in everything, and hardly records a permanent state (*Letters*, II, 217). Joyce simply did not want, as he said, to codify himself. But though he accepted Stanislaus's criticism that his socialism was thin and unsteady (*Letters*, II, 187), Joyce's ready imaginative sympathy for ordinary people made a socialist predisposition his lifelong basic political intuition. The attitudes that for a while coalesced as socialism remained fundamental to his cast of mind.

Associated with Joyce's socialism, as a reported outburst of 1906 makes clear (*Letters*, II, 151), is the pacifistic attitude to violence evident throughout his work, from an early positive view of Buddhism ('it refuses to make the battlefield the test of excellence', (*CW*, 94)), to the *Finnegans Wake* portrait of Shem. From the Professor Jones/Wyndham Lewis viewpoint of 'Shem the Penman', pacifism is cowardice, but this violent and racist viewpoint, from which Shem appears a 'Menschavik' (185), condemns itself: Joyce combines self-irony with an indirect ratification of Shem values. In *A Portrait of the Artist* Father

Dolan's assault on Stephen (a trauma remembered in *Ulysses* (458/561)), and the sadistic sermon on what Joyce, in his 'Portrait' essay, called the obscene idea of Hell, make violence disgusting. Stephen's refusal to sign Czar Nicholas II's International Peace Petition is not at odds with this: Stephen is opposed not to peace but to the petition. It is shallowly conceived ('If we must have a Jesus, let us have a legitimate Jesus'), and Stephen cannot associate himself with muddled moral gestures (the nationalist, Davin, signs, but keeps his Fenian arms manual). By the time Joyce wrote *A Portrait* the failure of the Hague Conference of 1899 to achieve the petition's main aim of disarmament, and the Russo–Japanese war of 1904–5 (which is in the background of *Ulysses*), had justified Stephen's scepticism. In *Ulysses* Joyce's hatred of violence is clearest in his transformation of the slaughter of the suitors (Ithaca), the implicit endorsement of Bloom in his confrontation with nationalist thuggery in Cyclops, and Stephen's parallel refusal to take on the British army in the person of Private Carr (Circe). Joyce's combination of socialism and pacifism means that he was never attracted, as were some of his former associates, by fascism (*Letters*, I, 227; III, 311).

With considerable reservations Joyce was also a nationalist – the reservations being his internationalist perspectives as a writer, his fear that an independent Ireland might be dominated by the Catholic Church, and the insistence in nationalist programmes on the Irish language (*Letters*, II, 187). 'Our island, Rome and duty!' (*FW*, 374) is the independence ethos that Joyce feared. Like his own creation, Gabriel Conroy (*Dubliners*), Joyce for a short time wrote reviews for the pro-Union *Daily Express* (an activity which earns Gabriel the taunt 'West Briton' from the nationalist Miss Ivors), but Joyce endorsed the policy of the *United Irishman* (*Letters*, II, 158), the Sinn Féin paper of Arthur Griffith, which began in 1899 by declaring its acceptance of the nationalism of '98, '48 and '67. For a while as a student Joyce read the paper every week.[5] Essays and lectures on Irish subjects written in 1907 for the Triestine Università Popolare and the newspaper *Il Piccolo della Sera* show Joyce continuing to follow

Anglo–Irish politics in detail. In 'Fenianism', 'Home Rule Comes of Age' (1907), and 'The Home Rule Comet' (1910) he supported Sinn Féin and the movement for Irish independence. At this time support for Sinn Féin did not mean endorsing violence, which would not at all have commanded Joyce's assent. In 1907 Sinn Féin meant a reformed Fenianism which 'no longer uses dynamite' (*CW*, 191). Its aim was to establish a bi-lingual republic and to bring this about by peaceful means: withdrawing from the British parliament, refusing the oath of allegiance to the Crown and service in the British army, while boycotting English goods, developing Irish industry, and trading without British intervention. This is the so-called 'Hungarian Policy' on which, in *Ulysses*, Arthur Griffith is advised by Bloom. And throughout *Ulysses* it is through Bloom more than Stephen – though the two are linked in their different radical and heterodox interests – that Joyce refracts his own politics: his socialism, his anti-clerical nationalism, and his opposition to revolutionary violence.

CULTURAL CONTEXTS[6]

For Joyce the most influential writers of the previous generation were, in the novel, Flaubert, and in the drama, Ibsen. From Flaubert Joyce learned his concern for style – not only the right words but, as he told Budgen, the right words in their perfect order.[7] Stephen's doctrine of the impersonality of the artist too is formulated in terms derived from Flaubert (*P*, 219; *CW*, 141). This aspect of Stephen's theorising does not come, as do most of Stephen's theories, directly from Joyce's own early essays and notebooks, though there is in the Paris notebook a related argument – also given to Stephen (*SH*, 72; *P*, 218) – describing a hierarchy of lyric, epic and dramatic in terms of increasing impersonality (*CW*, 145). The Flaubert theory's supposition of an indifferent author gives to the novel the impersonal quality Joyce admired in drama. Judgement of the significance of

Stephen's theory in *A Portrait* depends on an estimate of the complex and subtle way in which Joyce leads the reader to place Stephen. In some degree the theory is Stephen's not Joyce's and Joyce is not what the theory demands, the indifferent presenter of his material, though Joyce's ways of guiding response are (except in *Stephen Hero*) always implicatory. But this ambivalence itself is comparable to Flaubert's: 'Madame Bovary n'a rien de vrai ... je n'y ai rien mis ni de mes sentiments ni de mon existence'; but, on another occasion, and more famously, 'Madame Bovary, c'est moi'.[8] Flaubert's fictional transpositions are different from Joyce's but with both there is a similar uncertain relation between author and character. Joyce's theory is not, therefore, directly similar to the unequivocal theory of the impersonality of the artist propounded by T. S. Eliot in 'Tradition and the Individual Talent' which became one of the central creeds of Pound–Eliot Modernism – though with Eliot too it is open to question how far the theory was a veil for the traumatic personal experience he wished to include obliquely in his poetry.

Ibsen is a more important influence on Joyce because his impact was both aesthetic and moral. The aesthetic influence relates, like that of Flaubert, to the issue of impersonality (*CW*, 65) – again ambiguously, since Ibsen's detached handling of his autobiographical figures is open to a range of views, especially his treatment of artist figures in plays which were of particular importance to Joyce, Solness in *The Master Builder* and Rubek in *When We Dead Awake*. Morally Joyce's praise of Ibsen was that 'he let in fresh air' (*CW*, 46). Ruthlessly questioning with himself about the egotism of the stance, he was a serious moral adventurer, as Joyce wished to be. 'Extravagant excursions into forbidden territory' Joyce called his own work (*JJ*, 265): there are permanently challenging aspects of Joyce's ethical – as of his stylistic – experimentation, and Ibsen helped him to focus and articulate these. For the young Joyce, Ibsen was a scandalous weapon against Catholic orthodoxy, as he appears in *Stephen Hero*, where Stephen evidently enjoys the paradox of defending him in terms derived from the Angelic Doctor. *Exiles* is a discussion drama in the true Ibsen manner: an argument on a moral issue, with contrasting points of view fully given and the audience left to judge, with implications about how to do so. There is no clearer index of the error of attempting to reclaim Joyce for Catholic orthodoxy than the idea that the play is a repudiation of Ibsenite ethics on individual freedom, and specifically on free love[9]. The presence of Ibsen in *Finnegans Wake*, and Herbert Gorman's account of Joyce's continued interest in Ibsen in the Thirties,[10] make the error of a supposed repudiation clear. The moderate demur about art and moral teaching in Joyce's early essay, 'Drama and Life' (*CW*, 43) – which in *Stephen Hero* Stephen exalts into a campaign – needs to be understood in the context of what it opposed: *Othello* seen as 'an object lesson in the passion of jealousy', *Ghosts* as teaching self-repression (*SH*, 32, 51). Stephen's attack is on 'criticism ... established upon homilies' (*SH*, 75) – criticism which perverts art to inculcate the morals of the interpreter – and on art which presents didactically a platitudinous morality. Joyce himself admired even didactic art when it presented a moral challenge, as with the stories of Tolstoy (*Letters*, I, 364). His doubts do not extend to morally revolutionary work in which ideas are presented by suggestion or treated in an investigative way, as by Ibsen. In Stephen's confrontation with the college authorities over his paper 'Art and Life' his ingenious insistence that aesthetics is the only issue becomes his alibi for dealing with morally advanced material. From its own point of view the Church rightly recognises that Ibsen is a dangerous writer, not because he is an aesthete, but because his work implies immoral morals about the emancipation of women, the egotism of traditional concepts of duty and self-abnegation, the Nietzschean new duty of individual self-realisation, and so forth. It is in part through the moral effect of writers such as Tolstoy and Ibsen that 'civilization may be said to be the creation of its outlaws' (*SH*, 160) – amongst whom Joyce hoped to number himself. 'I seriously believe', he wrote to Grant Richards about the publication of *Dubliners*, 'that you will retard the course of civilisation in Ireland by preventing the Irish people from

having one good look at themselves in my nicely polished
looking-glass' (*Letters*, I, 64). And to Nora, in words later echoed
by Stephen, 'I am one of the writers of this generation who are
perhaps creating at last a conscience in the soul of this wretched
race' (*Letters*, II, 311; *P*, 257).

Joyce's attitude to his Irish Renaissance contemporaries, most
fully indicated by the Scylla and Charybdis episode of *Ulysses*,
is summed up in 'The Holy Office': 'That they may dream their
dreamy dreams/I carry off their filthy streams' (*CW*, 151). The
one exception to Joyce's general denigration of the
'Yogibogeybox' group (*U*, 157/191) is Yeats. Joyce liked to poke
fun at him. In *Ulysses* Yeats is subjected to Buck Mulligan's
best wit (Bloom is still chuckling over it when he goes to bed
(178/216, 346/424, 580/706)). In *Finnegans Wake* he is 'Will-
of-the-Wisp' (211); Shaun's geomater satirises the diagrams of
A Vision (293–5). Yeats was antithetical to Joyce in his politics
(he wrote marching songs for General O'Duffy's fascist blue-
shirts – 'the O'Daffy' Joyce calls him in *Finnegans Wake*); in
his apocalyptic view of history (Yeats's gyres have nothing in
common, beyond cyclicality, with the Viconian cycles which
Joyce used as one basis for the *Wake*); and in his attachment
to histories and myths of heroic failure (Emmet; Cuchulain –
the reverse of Joyce's resurrecting Finnegan). Joyce's seedy
urban realism is a kind of answer to Yeats's idealising picture
of an authentic rural Ireland of aristocrats and peasants, heroic
myth and widely disseminated imaginative legend. Joyce and
Yeats offer competing versions of Ireland and, beyond that,
competing versions of what it is to be human, as Yeats
acknowledged by attacking Joyce in the first edition of *A Vision*
(1926): Joyce is an example of the fractured modern
consciousness against which his own work strove. The contrast
between Yeats and Joyce highlights the distinctive qualities of
each: they are antithetical, but Joyce admired Yeats, probably
beyond any of his contemporaries (*JJ*, 660). The other near-
contemporary Irish writer important to Joyce, but in this case
important by association, is Wilde. Tried for a sexual crime, in
Finnegans Wake he is analogous to the Bloom figure, HCE. On

sexuality, Joyce's essay on Wilde is tailored to evade the prejudices of its Italian Catholic audience, but it is clear that, for Joyce, Wilde was a fellow socialist (in 1909 Joyce proposed translating *The Soul of Man Under Socialism* into Italian (*JJ*, 274)), a fellow exile, and a type of Joyce's own favourite role, the rebellious artist betrayed to the mob, specifically a scapegoat for English puritanism (*CW*, 204).

That there are significant similarities between Joyce and other Modernists is plain: a new sense of character as less fixed and less purely individual described in Virginia Woolf's essays[11] and embodied in her novels and those of Dorothy Richardson; following from this, experiments with rendering consciousness, especially the interior monologue or so-called 'stream-of-consciousness' technique[12]; a text more open in its variety of discourses and in its discreet and unfixed symbolism; the development of non-narrative structures and a use of myth which have obvious affinities with *The Waste Land* and with Pound's *Cantos*. It is distorting, though, to see Joyce too readily in the light of the Pound–Eliot version of Modernism. Much of what is most interesting and characteristic in Joyce's work is obscured by this context. Even where there are similarities, mutual sympathy was often partial. The Odysseus myth behind *Ulysses* is central too to the *Cantos*, but Joyce and Pound use the myth to embody quite different attitudes. With Pound the myth remains, in the obvious sense, heroic; and, in keeping with his anti-usurious ethics, his heroes are pre-bourgeois. Similarly, the language experiments in the later parts of *Ulysses* and throughout *Finnegans Wake* are paralleled in the *Cantos*, where the untranslatability of languages is constantly enacted as an index of how language constructs the world which on a simpler view it is taken to reflect. But Pound thought ill of *Finnegans Wake*, and for the primary formal revolution of Pound's poetry – breaking the pentameter (Canto 81) – Joyce's sympathy seems to have been distinctly limited.[13] And beyond these partial similarities and limited sympathies there are overt differences in politics, in religion, in aesthetics and on issues of gender. In religion Joyce was a post-Enlightenment sceptic whose Catholic training coloured his thought to a degree that is still, and probably ever shall be, a matter of controversy. Joyce's lifelong dialogue with the Catholic Church was an antagonistic one, as he announced in an early letter to Nora: 'I make open war upon it by what I write and say and do' (*Letters*, II, 48). The most one can say of his later attitudes is that he was, like Shem, 'of twosome twiminds forenenst gods' (*FW*, 188), but this does not mean that he was ever reconciled to Catholicism. 'I couldn't do that to him' Nora declined, when a priest offered his services for Joyce's funeral (*JJ*, 742). As Jaun/Shaun has it (he is trying to free Dave the Dancekerl/Shem from emotional reticence and sexual inhibition), 'there's no plagues like rome' (*FW*, 465). On Protestantism Joyce was unequivocal. Frank Budgen records from Joyce's conversation the verdict with which Stephen is endowed: unlike the logical and coherent absurdity, Catholicism, it is an absurdity illogical and incoherent[14]. Joyce moved, therefore, in precisely the opposite direction from T. S. Eliot, and took none of the interest in alternative religions shown by Yeats, Lawrence and Pound.

Nor can Joyce be grouped with Pound/Eliot/Hulme Modernism in his admiration for Romantic art, as in his lecture on 'the most enlightened of Western poets', Blake (*CW*, 75, 214–22), the important invocations of Byron and Shelley in *A Portrait*, and his high praise of Wordsworth.[15] In *Finnegans Wake*, with Joyce's usual self-irony – a basic sympathy conscious of humorous possibilities – Shem moulds himself on Wagner and Shelley (229–31), while Professor Jones neurotically condemns Romanticism ('impulsivism') out of what a Freudian would call reaction formation (149, 151). The 'classical temper' which Stephen exalts in *Stephen Hero* as 'a constant state of the artistic mind' (73–4) is a good account of one side of Joyce's own work. But Stephen's sense that materialism is a danger inherent in the classical is endorsed by the Scylla and Charybdis episode of *Ulysses*: Stephen may sail nearer the rock/Aristotle/ materialism than the whirlpool/Plato/idealism, but either could be fatal. The classical temper is at odds with an important aspect of Stephen's artistic personality (*SH*, 188), and it registers only one aspect of Joyce's mind. His whole attitude Joyce articulated most fully in relation to the nineteenth-century Irish poet, James Clarence Mangan: the struggles of classic and romantic against their own inherent corruptions and against each other show an unrest which 'is the condition of all achievement ... and presses slowly towards a deeper insight which will make the schools at one' (*CW*, 74).

One concept which can be seen as connecting Joyce both with other Modernists and with the Romantic tradition is the epiphany. Stephen propounds the theory: the epiphany is 'a sudden spiritual manifestation, whether in the vulgarity of speech or of gesture or in a memorable phase of the mind itself' (*SH*, 188). The term itself, derived from the manifestation of Christ to the Magi, and Stephen's alternative reference to the Eucharist (*SH*, 33), connect the epiphany with Stephen's quasi-religious conception of the artist as a 'priest of the eternal imagination', though the extant epiphanies are nonrational, intuitive, emotional, rather than in any strict sense 'spiritual'. Stephen's account indicates that the epiphanies are of two kinds: objective, recording precisely the surface of some indicative moment but with no authorial indication of its significance; and subjective, recreating the impressions of a particular perceiving mind. Morris Beja rightly suggests that with the extant epiphanies the divisions dramatic/lyrical and dialogue/narrative would be equally accurate.[16] In themselves the epiphanies are open, even inscrutable texts, but even in Stephen's plan they are not intended as discrete pieces: they are to be a collection; they will interact with and comment on one another like a book of prose poems, or like the stories of *Dubliners*. In his published work Joyce always expanded and contextualised them in ways that point and delimit significance. The epiphany which in *Stephen Hero* gives rise to the theory is fragmentary in the extreme. Divorced from its context it would be susceptible of any number of meanings. In *Stephen Hero* it has clear keynotes of religion, guilt and spiritual paralysis. This movement towards increased specificity of significance can be traced in every major adaptation of epiphany fragments into a context intended for publication. Joyce's first task with the epiphanies was to record commonplace moments that he saw as containing deeper significance. His second was to discover and communicate that significance, not in a way that closed off all variety of meaning, but not either without implying meanings.

There has been considerable argument over the importance of the epiphanies to Joyce. He collected them very seriously as a young man, though he never described the theory in his published work. Stephen mocks the youthful pretentiousness of their importance to him in *Ulysses* (34/40), but Joyce reworked them into *A Portrait*, *Ulysses*, and *Finnegans Wake*, and he uses the concept with his usual comic seriousness in the *Wake*'s climactic confrontation (611) which is 'defence and indictment of the book itself' (*Letters*, I, 406). The epiphany connects Joyce with other Modernists: these sudden transformations of the ordinary are comparable to Virginia Woolf's 'moments of being', to the moments in and out of time of Eliot's *Four Quartets*, to 'the fourth dimension, stillness' central to Pound's *Cantos* (XLIX). And there are formal as well as conceptual similarities: the indeterminacy of the fragments, and their use as key elements in non-narrative structuration (though the only work in which Joyce uses the epiphany as the dominant principle of organisation is the posthumously published *Giacomo Joyce*). But the epiphany equally connects Joyce with Romanticism. 'Kubla Khan' is only the most obvious example of that Romantic open text, the constructed ruin. The artist as 'priest of the eternal imagination', a quasi-religious being opposed to the priest of sect and dogma, is a thoroughly Romantic figure. And how to construct a large-scale work without narrative was precisely Wordsworth's problem in *The Prelude*. His solution was to organise his portrait of the artist around crucial moments of heightened consciousness which he called 'spots of time': it is the epiphany under another name.

Critical Reception:
Theoretical Perspectives

Joyce's extraordinary imagination for experiment and innovation in form and language is undoubted. The nature and quality of the vision this served is in every aspect controversial. Joyce is in some degree a realist, a symbolist, an ironist and a mythographer, but the fundamental meanings of his work depend on the very different ways in which these elements can be understood and combined. Joyce can be seen as an Enlightenment rationalist fallen among Catholics, or as maintaining, despite his loss of faith, an essentially Catholic perspective; as a humanist, or as attacking humanist views of the individual, art and language. These different readings of Joyce are a proper reflection of the scope of his work: it provides ample material for widely divergent emphases. Some of these can be combined. Some cannot, and the most basic issues of moral, intellectual and literary value are involved in the contest of perspectives.

Of the earliest studies of *Ulysses* those of Pound (1922), Eliot (1923), Edmund Wilson (1931) and Wyndham Lewis (1927) raise central critical issues – about the kind of work *Ulysses* is, and its view of the world. Pound emphasised Joyce's debt to Flaubert as a stylist and praised his realism, praise which is in keeping with Joyce's practice in writing and the critical principles reflected in his letters and recorded conversations.[1] Eliot praised Joyce for his quasi-scientific discovery of a new way to structure works using myth, and gathered Joyce into his waste-land grumbling about the modern world. Eliot was soon to discover

Ulysses

in Anglo–Catholicism and firm social hierarchies a cure for the modern world's ills which is not obviously in keeping with Joyce's declared allegiances: for Joyce 'it is sinful foolishness to sigh back for the good old times ... Life we must accept as we see it before our eyes' (*CW*, 45). Edmund Wilson's *Axel's Castle*, a book with a European frame of reference, while acknowledging Joyce's debt to Flaubert, drew out his connection with Symbolist theory and practice and so combined something of Pound's and Eliot's perspectives. Joyce's precise recording of Dublin surfaces indicates, though, how much the Symbolist influence is combined (as it is not by other writers in Wilson's account) with a more traditional novelistic realism. The nature and importance of this combination of realistic surface with mythic or symbolic resonance remains a permanent issue for every reader of Joyce.

Wyndham Lewis saw a different Joyce from either Pound or Eliot, and deplored what he saw. *Time and Western Man* is an attack on the relativistic world view which derives from Bergson in philosophy and Einstein in physics. Together, for Lewis, they produce a dead, mechanistic view of the world. Joyce, along with other Modernists, is held to demonstrate the effects of this for art. Joyce's characters are clichés, his Irish subjects are parochial, his brilliance is entirely of technique and this obscures fundamentally commonplace attitudes. Joyce is a craftsman, not a creator. It is a view Joyce himself entertained when he doubted his imaginative powers (*JJ*, 660), the view of D. H. Lawrence, the view that led F. R. Leavis to exclude Joyce from his 'great tradition' and the view that is elaborated by Arnold Kettle (1961). Joyce thought Lewis the best of his hostile critics (*Letters*, III, 250) and answered his attack in *Finnegans Wake*. There Lewis is caricatured as the spokesman of commonsense ('the beast of boredom' (292)) opposed to Joyce's technical experiments (Lewis was in fact hardly this at all), but Joyce did attempt to identify the issues behind Lewis's critique, though for him these were not Bergson and Einstein. Joyce associated Lewis with the viewpoint of the *Wake*'s portrait of its main Joyce figure, Shem.[2] This is an indictment of its speaker, a militarist, racist (attacking Jews and blacks), Hitler-fancier and KKK supporter, who recognises Shem/Joyce as a Communist, in line with Joyce's later criticism of Lewis's politics, which included support for Hitler until shortly before the Second World War.

Like the Pound and Eliot essays, the early books on *Ulysses* by Stuart Gilbert (1930) and Frank Budgen (1934), though both writers were assisted by Joyce, explicitly emphasised different qualities of the novel.[3] Answering criticisms of the novel's formlessness, Gilbert stressed the Homeric parallels and technical innovations. Gilbert did not meet Joyce until 1927, but Budgen knew Joyce well from 1918, and his book records conversations with Joyce when *Ulysses* was work in progress. Budgen stresses the novel's characterisation and human content over aspects of technique on the grounds that in conversations with Joyce these were Joyce's own priorities.

A different debate is epitomised by the opposed views of Hugh Kenner (1956) and Richard Ellmann (1972). Ethically Kenner presents a Catholic's Joyce, with an excellent knowledge of the sources of Joyce's thought in Aquinas, though Kenner's attitude to this is hardly that of Joyce himself at any stage of his life. Aesthetically Kenner's view is anti-Romantic: Joyce as seen by Poundian Modernism. And though T. S. Eliot is not invoked, his notion of a dissociation of sensibility is evidently at work: the Kenner view is an elaboration of Eliot's comment that *Ulysses* shows 'the immense panorama of futility and anarchy which is contemporary history' (1923). Kenner expands Wyndham Lewis's 'brilliant misreading': Lewis was right in his description, wrong only in thinking the mind of the book is the mind of Joyce. It is a mind Joyce is recording and exposing, the mechanistic mind of the modern world. The nineteenth century comes in for particularly rough treatment as the nadir before the Modernist dawn: it shows the effects of the Enlightenment in religion and the French Revolution in politics – scepticism and democracy. The Homeric parallels of *Ulysses* are a way of commenting on the decay of modern life. Bloom is the Enlightenment in a mocking mirror. Molly is the flesh:

she kills the soul, darkens the intellect, and blunts the moral
sense. *Ulysses* is an *Inferno*. Kenner's view of Stephen is
especially indicative. Stephen is a parody of Joyce, a futile *alter
ego* who has more in common with the feckless Jimmy Doyle
(of 'After the Race') than with his author. When Stephen is a
severe classicist, burning his poems, he may be identified with
Joyce; when he is a Romantic, Joyce is criticising him. But
Joyce's own tastes were not for Stravinsky and neo-classicism:
they were for Schoeck and late-Romanticism. Joyce published
his own Romantic poems which, though they enact some of
Pound's formulae, are in their total effect utterly unlike Pound.
The 'morbidminded esthete and embryo philosopher' view of
Stephen is presented in *Ulysses*, but hardly from an outlook
(T. H. Huxley's) we are invited to accept (343/420). The complex
Stephen/Joyce relationship is less easily sorted than Kenner
pretends. Kenner's Joyce is as coldly inhuman towards life as
he finds it as the Stephen of Kenner's account whom he is
supposed to reject. In the preface to a recent new edition (1987)
Kenner retracts his view of Bloom and of Molly, but not of
Stephen: it is on an ironic view of Stephen that the Catholic
reading depends. But what, then, of the analogy between Stephen
and Bloom that Kenner puts at the head of 'How to read
Ulysses'? Kenner's retraction calls in question more than he
wishes, but his *Dublin's Joyce* remains the most powerful, subtle
and intelligent expression of a fundamentally mistaken vision
of Joyce.[4]

   From different basic perspectives Richard Ellmann and S. L.
Goldberg put an opposite view. Ellmann's is a humanist's Joyce.
For him the Homeric parallels, despite obvious comic discrep-
ancies, do not undercut: they exalt. Bloom is, in his way, a
worthy Odysseus. Ellmann also elicits from *Ulysses* various
moral propositions: Joyce is a moralist, but one who works by
implication, leaving the reader to formulate. Centrally, Ellmann
presents *Ulysses* as schematic in ways not made evident by
Joyce's schemata (Ellmann presents his own). The novel's
episodes are arranged in triads which present thesis, antithesis
and synthesis. The whole has a fourfold meaning analogous to

the traditional levels of scriptural interpretation. The meanings of *Ulysses* are literal (narrative), ethical (discriminating between desirable and undesirable life), aesthetic (presenting a relationship between art and nature), and anagogic (concerned with the ultimate justification of existence). Ellmann had a fine sense of Joyce's values and his scholarship was unrivalled. One can accept this while still seeing *Ulysses* as anarchically at odds with his schematisations. S. L. Goldberg (1961) propounds both a different answer to Kenner and – from a fundamentally Leavisite position – an answer to the Lawrence/Leavis objections that beneath the technical inventiveness Joyce's view of life is trivial. Goldberg, who is well aware of his Leavisite presuppositions (and of the bases of other views, on which he makes interesting and provocative remarks), allows these to interact with Joyce, not, as in some more aggressively theoretical criticism, to dictate what becomes visible. Goldberg's account of Stephen's aesthetic theories as they are placed by their contexts draws out significances which are not purely aesthetic: contextualised, the apparently art-for-art's-sake theories are not incompatible with moral meanings of a kind required by Goldberg's presuppositions. His overarching theme is that classicism is a technical discipline, but it is not just an artistic procedure: underlying it, and essential to it, is a moral attitude, 'a belief that man's desire will always reach beyond the limits of his imperfections but that even in the darkest places he may still proceed balanced between *hubris* and despair' (118). On this view, Joyce's classicism is not at odds with the Romantic rebellion, the struggles to reach beyond limits of imperfection, that his work embodies. On the contrary, it is part of the answer to Kenner that Kenner misrepresents Joyce's attitude by misunderstanding his irony: only in part satiric, it is complex with compassion and endorsement. Goldberg's own weakness is to see the technical experiments of the later parts of *Ulysses* as at odds with the vision of life he adduces so well: on a different view of language they are perfectly continuous with it, and it is precisely a different view of language that is a central element in contemporary criticism.

While Goldberg applied to Joyce assumptions generated largely by pre-Modernist texts, recent criticism has been partly generated by Joyce's own work, particularly by the language experiments of the later parts of *Ulysses* and *Finnegans Wake*. A representative apologist for neoteric views is Colin MacCabe. His *James Joyce and the Revolution of the Word* draws on the ideas on authors and narrative of Roland Barthes, on language of Saussure, Julia Kristeva and Jacques Derrida, and on the revised Freudian psychoanalysis of Jacques Lacan.[5] In MacCabe's account Joyce's fictions are not to be interpreted in terms of theme: they investigate the processes of writing and reading, and their significances emerge from that investigation. What MacCabe represents as the failed attempts of earlier criticism to grapple with Joyce show the inadequacy of its categories: author, seen as producer of meaning; reader, seen as a unified and passive receiver; language, seen as referring to a world beyond itself. The classic realist novel of George Eliot shows the classic misconceptions of criticism at work. The issue here is the position of the author, whose death had been announced by Barthes, and whose dissolution had been insinuated by Foucault.[6] In George Eliot there is a hierarchy of discourses: all the voices are placed by a narrative voice which closes off alternative interpretations and offers a single correct meaning. The passive reader knows what to think and so is 'comfortable'. These 'neurotic texts' are to be treated as an analyst treats a patient. The advanced reader reads against the narrative voice: fissures show what is suppressed – that is, detail is wrested from defining contexts to undermine evident meanings, and the text is dislocated into meaning what the interpreter wishes. But readers who feel comfortable with George Eliot because they know where they are morally must be morally perfect or morally obtuse. Colin MacCabe (waiving pride of intellect, which peeps occasionally from his page) is no doubt perfect, but for every comfortable reader who is perfect there will be ninety-nine who are, as George Eliot puts it, 'well wadded with stupidity'. Readers who recognise their kinship with imperfection will not find knowing where they are morally with George Eliot so comfortable. As for the MacCabe view of language as non-referential play, it would certainly have perplexed Joyce who worried that *Dubliners* had not adequately reflected the city's ethos and prided himself that Dublin could be physically reconstructed from *Ulysses*.[7]

That Joyce's texts are radically different from George Eliot's MacCabe argues by means of the *Dubliners* story, 'Ivy Day in the Committee Room'. No authorial voice establishes a perspective, so if we attempt to look at the story in terms of theme we cannot choose between opposed meanings. While with the classic realist text we act like an analyst, with Joyce the absence of governing perspective means that we act like an analysand: we are forced to interrogate our own discourses. Reading Joyce is do-it-yourself Lacanian analysis. But you do not have to supply examples of authorial discourse to situate an authorial position. It is impossible for an author wholly to withdraw from a text because, as Wayne Booth argues, everything an author shows will serve to tell: the author can only choose his or her disguises.[8]

More helpful than MacCabe on play of discourse is Mikhail Bakhtin. Bakhtin's ideas on the carnival nature of comedy and on the dialogic nature of language – that all uses of language refer explicitly or implicitly to some other use – though developed in the Stalinist Soviet Union possibly in ignorance of Joyce, are virtually a description of what Joyce was doing. Bakhtin rightly argues that the author's view can be gauged by the nature of the intersection of competing discourses.[9] So it is with Joyce. MacCabe's anti-thematic view ignores the fact that 'Ivy Day' is a story in a sequence, that what it means is determined partly by its place in the sequence, that other stories in *Dubliners* are more morally explicit, and that Joyce himself assigned the whole collection a moral significance (*Letters*, II, 134). MacCabe applies the same technique to the Cyclops episode of *Ulysses* with the same evasion of how its meaning is determined by relation to other parts of the novel. That Joyce intended the episode to have moral meanings of the kind his letters identify in *Dubliners* is clear from his preparatory notesheets.[10] MacCabe converts Joyce'e obliquity, his desire for

the reader to discover meanings, into an assertion that there is
no meaning to discover. An argument about narrative corresponds with that about play of discourse: by moving towards
closure and a position of knowledge narrative represses desire;
narrative disruption liberates. Narrative closure is associated
arbitrarily with the masculine (Balzac and Freud adduced,
George Eliot forgotten), narrative disruption with the feminine,
and a supposed sexual politics of Joyce's forms is constructed
from this on the unargued and too easy assumption that formal
disruption and the politically disruptive are conterminous.

MacCabe's sources are variously Joycean, but in ways more
open to speculation than his use of them suggests. In linguistics
since Saussure, central issues relevant to Joyce's experiments
with language have been the arbitrary nature of the linguistic
sign, its establishing of meaning only by differential relation to
other terms, and the problematic relationship between language,
consciousness and the world summed up in the Heideggerian
tag, *die Sprache spricht* – language, not the speaker, creates
meaning. In the work of Derrida the Saussurean establishing of
meaning by relation gives rise to an idea of meaning as
perpetually deferred, never fully present. This is accompanied
by a sense of language as irreducibly polysemous (Joyce's
experiments are an acknowledged presence here), and a deconstructive reading concentrating on paradoxes or apparent con-
tradictions which allow a text to be read against authorial
intention. Nietzsche's death of God, which led to the analogous
death of the author as controller of meaning, and his notion of
truth as a rhetorical device designed to exclude undesired
meanings, have offered further bases, outside linguistics, for
interpretative freedom. Nietzsche's attack on truth is one ground
of various anti-rationalist discourses: the ludic aspects of
Derrida's texts; Heidegger's attempts to prise thought away
from an identification with logic. A related sense of logic as
repressive, and a problematising of the relation between speech
and writing of evident relevance to Joyce, lies behind the
associatively organised transcribed lectures and seminars of
Lacan. The attack on truth is also one ground of Foucault's

challenge to the languages and organising categories of history, which, in the area of sexuality, bears on Modernist texts in their questionings of gender. This issue has been foregrounded too in feminist analyses examining both explicit sexual ideologies and those implicit in a text's presentation of sex roles or its formal and linguistic features. These and associated lines of thought decentre the autonomous individual, who is reconstructed as, in large measure – perhaps entirely – a site constituted by transindividual forces, over which the problematic nature of language gives, at best, limited consciousness, and over which consciousness, driven by inner and outer forces it can hardly see, has, at best, limited control.

Not all of this is entirely new. *Pace* the standard caricature of anti-humanist critique, humanism promoted language-learning because it recognised that different languages construct experience differently. That the individual was entirely autonomous nobody with any sense of history could ever have believed. Precisely the opposite is one reason for the humanist study of culturally remote texts: you may recognise common experiences within different systems of value; you also learn how profoundly other being human might be in a different cultural situation. And well before institutionalised criticism as it now exists began, Darwin, Marx, and Freud had destabilised authorial control of meaning, in that all give reasons for supposing that there might be more in a text than its author or first audience could recognise. A text will exemplify a stage in the evolution of forms (a stage that can be fully understood only in terms of futures to which it gives rise); it will express its society's means of production (in which the first audience is also enmeshed); it will express its author's subconscious, and address the subconscious of its readers. This does not, either, overthrow previous methods of criticism, though it is often part of its rhetorical strategy to claim it does. Everywhere there are continuities. Deconstruction is a (repudiated) child of Empsonian ambiguity and multiple meaning. Lacanian psychoanalysis offers a disruptive portrait of the father, Freud, but he is reclaimed, not cast off. Language can still be supposed to refer to the world: indeed it can be seen as the trope of an anti-political discourse to pretend otherwise. The whole Heideggerian style is designed to disrupt the tendency of language to govern meaning by its own logic, while Heidegger's etymological probings are an attempt to create, or recover, a language which is not emptied of significance by conventional usage but which has some kind of incarnational relation, usually metaphoric, to what it names. These *nouvelles critiques* do not dispose of traditional modes of interpretation, though in some areas these now appear newly problematic. With respect to Joyce the most valuable perspectives that recent critical theories suggest relate to issues of language, gender and the nature of the individual.

II

ULYSSES
A Reading of the Text

1

Themes and Techniques

The initial difficulties of reading *Ulysses* lie in establishing from its profusion of detail recurrent centres of interest, and in understanding the relation of stylistic experiment in each episode to subject-matter. Though Joyce's detail can be dazzling and his formal experiments bewildering, it is by accretion of detail that Joyce defines his subjects and in his inventiveness with form and language that much of the pleasure of reading him lies. There is a constant tension in Joyce between pattern-making and the proliferation of detail which explodes pattern and tends to the chaotic. The first is evident in Joyce's schemata for *Ulysses* (see Appendix), the second in his revisions of both *Ulysses* and *Finnegans Wake*; but schemata and revisions simply provide physical evidence of what is clear in *Ulysses* itself. Criticism needs to keep both poles in view, not taming Joyce's prolific inventiveness, not losing the centres of *Ulysses* in the delights of its detail. Creative disruption of conventions of perception and expression is part of Joyce's aim, and criticism must not, by normalising, work ultimately against these disruptions. But disruption is confusing, not creative, unless it works from points of contact with convention, as Joyce acknowledged in reserving the more radical experiments of *Ulysses* for later episodes, and in the bridge-building criticism he sponsored for both *Ulysses* and *Finnegans Wake*. Synopsising from a novel so various inevitably falsifies, and so I have retained in the commentary the boundaries of Joyce's structure, discussing central issues of theme and form in the way that these arise, episode by episode, indicating more randomly, with some favourite examples, the variety of ways in which Joycean detail works. Even working with Joyce's structure the convenient separation of theme and form is artificial. The reading experience of many episodes is, and remains, primarily of their formal experimentation. The reader asks first, and continues to ask, not 'What is this about?' but, the more basic though finally inseparable question, 'What is this use of language doing?'. Joyce's form often is his theme, but not the whole of his theme, nor so often as the obsessions of some contemporary criticism would have it.

Reference to the *Odyssey* in *Ulysses* is continuous, but it is various in kind, and can be seen in different ways. Joyce himself used the Homeric titles of each episode in conversation and correspondence, and though they were not included in the novel they have traditionally provided a convenient mode of reference in criticism. Some Homeric bases of *Ulysses* are of minor importance in the *Odyssey* itself. Some are matters of detail in *Ulysses*. Joyce finds humorous 'equivalents' for many aspects of Homeric myth and action: the Cyclops' rock hurled after Odysseus/the citizen's biscuit tin thrown at Bloom; the herb Moly, which protects Odysseus against Circe/Bloom's talismanic potato; Odysseus kissing the earth on his return to Ithaca/Bloom, on his return to Eccles Street, kissing Molly (his Gea-Tellus) on the buttocks. That is, ghostly Homeric presences are a source of jokes. Homer is also a source of the novel's basic structure of journey and return/reunion, and of many central elements of its subject-matter and themes. Whether the characters are measured in terms of a heroic backdrop and found wanting, or the heightenings of heroic myth are found to have genuine, though at first surprising, correspondences in ordinary life, is a question to which there is no simple or single answer.

I   TELEMACHIA

1.   Telemachus (Odyssey, I)

The Telemachia as a whole introduces, with reference to Stephen, many of the main issues of *Ulysses*. Telemachus concerns Stephen's relations with two masters: with England in politics; with Ireland in religion and in art. His immediate personal relationships are emblematic. Haines represents an aspect of England, placed partly by his anti-Semitism, partly by his comfortable attitude to Ireland: if 'history is to blame' he personally is not implicated. Mulligan is more complex. Stephen shares many of his attitudes. Both read Wilde, Swinburne, Nietzsche and Whitman, the artistic, intellectual and sexual rebels of the previous generation. Both read (though only Mulligan mocks) Yeats. Like Mulligan, Stephen can be wittily blasphemous, but Mulligan's lively mockery of religion is tainted: it is a reflex response, an attitude in which he is stuck. Mulligan epitomises for Joyce an Irish attitude to Ireland. Haines is Ireland's conqueror. Mulligan is her 'gay betrayer'. Many of Joyce's characters – vivid and convincing simply in terms of realism – are of this kind: suggestive of more than themselves. With the old milkwoman of Telemachus Stephen spells this out – she is Ireland: 'Silk of the kine and poor old woman, names given her in old times'. As Ireland she provokes characteristic reactions. Mulligan mocks her religion. Haines expects her to be romantically picturesque, speaking Gaelic – a nationalist issue because English was the language of the conqueror. Joyce tried for a while to learn Gaelic (*JJ*, 61), as does Stephen (*P*, 206). The Joyce figure in 'The Dead', Gabriel Conroy, is berated as a West Briton for his ignorance of the language. But as the milkwoman's comic non-recognition indicates – 'Is it French you are talking, sir?' – Gaelic was learned by the intelligentsia. Outside the rural West it was not widely spoken. The comedy here is an early index of the presentation of inward-looking aspects of nationalism developed most fully in Cyclops.

The first episodes revolve around Stephen's character and the themes this articulates. Deeply disturbed by his mother's death, he is not simply what mocker Mulligan would provoke him to be. In Stephen's memories of his mother's daily life and of objects she saved to memorialise special occasions, in the pathos of her inevitably defeated resistance to time, Joyce evokes basic feelings about death which Stephen cannot avoid but which his

own needs for independence force him to struggle against: his
mother's influence would pull him back to the Church. The
legacy of Stephen's crucial act of resistance to his mother, his
refusal to pray at her request while she was dying, is the most
emotionally pressing aspect of his general problem: how to free
himself from the grip of the Church. One other main aspect of
Stephen announced in Telemachus is his *Hamlet* theory.
Mourning a parent, isolated, moody and bitterly humorous,
emphatically dressed in black, even living in a fortification that
makes Haines think of Elsinore, Stephen is not just exhibiting
in the theory his gift for aggressive intellectual pyrotechnics.
The play suits his emotional situation. A dispossessed
Telemachus (he pays the rent; Mulligan takes the key), he is
also a usurped Hamlet to whom Mulligan–Claudius is
superficially friendly but fundamentally antagonistic. Stephen's
Hamlet theory, as the common thread with his theological
imaginings underlines, also extracts from the play another of
his central preoccupations – and a main theme of the novel:
the relation of fathers to sons.

2. *Nestor (Odyssey, III)*

Nestor shows Stephen subject through economic necessity to
the wisdom of Mr Deasy, the wisdom of an old age that has
never been young. Like Mulligan the betrayer, Mr Deasy
characterises an aspect of Ireland. He is an Ulster Protestant
Unionist who admires England for the most materialist of
reasons. His vision of English greatness is summed up in the
Englishman's 'proudest boast': '*I paid my way*'. It has all the
spiritual grandeur of professor MacHugh's epitome of English
imperialist mentality: '*It is meet to be here. Let us construct a
watercloset*' (108/131). From this perspective Stephen, as a
disaffected young man from a Catholic background, appears a
Fenian. It is a perception which tells us nothing about Stephen,
for whom revolutionary nationalism has no appeal, but much
about the fantasies on which the internal animosities of Ireland
are built. Mr Deasy also has fantasies about Jews: like Haines

he is an anti-Semite, an attitude for which he finds a sanction in religion. Mr Deasy prepares us for Bloom's isolation: anti-Jewish feeling is rife in the Protestant as in the Catholic community. Joyce presents a quite different view in Stephen's thoughts of the Jewish community in Paris (28/34), all of which seems prophetic in a novel published in 1922, though it is also historically accurate for 1904. The Jews Stephen saw in Paris had been schooled on the instability of their position by the Dreyfus affair.

The main underlying thread of Nestor is History. Mr Deasy proclaims a philosophy of history – he is a Hegelian: 'All human history moves towards one great goal, the manifestation of God.' Stephen muses on alternatives: the determinist debate framed in terms suggested by Aristotle; an apocalyptic view which he derives from Blake; and perhaps the cyclical (even as a street name Vico invokes the notion of recurrent patterns in history which is basic to *Finnegans Wake*). The history Stephen teaches is plainer fare: names, dates, places, events and one-liners ('*Another victory like that and we are done for*'). Even when such history is not (as much of Mr Deasy's is) prejudice based on misinformation, it is a kind of fiction, 'a tale like any other'. But there is another history, not of characters and narrative like the nineteenth-century novel, but one better reflected by the techniques of Modernism. This is history as it is conveyed in Pound's *Cantos* through indicative fragments which correspond both to the Poundian Imagist tenets and to the epiphanies of Joyce's fiction.

> Glorious, pious and immortal memory. The lodge of Diamond in Armagh the splendid behung with corpses of papishes. Hoarse, masked and armed, the planters' covenant. The black north and true blue bible. Croppies lie down. (26/31)

An Orange toast to William III; a massacre of 1795; an oath of loyalty to the English crown rewarded with gifts of land which had then to be held by violence; the Ulster Protestant Tory alliance; a Unionist song celebrating the killing of the Wexford Catholic rebels of 1798: this is history lived on the pulses. But in whatever form, Ireland's past operates powerfully in shaping its present. It is the nightmare of being dragged down by this shaping force that Stephen is trying to evade.

3. Proteus (Odyssey, IV, 347–570)

Proteus is a shape-changer, an incarnation of the instability of the physical world. Stephen's perception of this links him with one of Bloom's preoccupations – metempsychosis – particularly when Stephen sees protean transformation in human terms. Proteus means continual birth. Stephen is a transformation of his father ('the man with my voice and my eyes'); in this sense all fathers and sons are consubstantial; and we are all transformations of mother Eve. Proteus also means continual death, and on this Stephen out-Hamlets Hamlet, having God go a progress through the guts of a fish (42, 478–9/50).[1] The difficulties of catching Proteus (to learn from him, as Menelaus does in Homer) lie not only in who he is but also in who we are – that is, in the nature of human perception: do we perceive an exterior world which is objectively there; or do we create what we suppose ourselves to perceive, and if so in what ways? Proteus shows Stephen thinking about this and experiencing it. Like the world it perceives, Stephen's mind is protean: it has been changed by time (Stephen looks back with self-irony on the person he once was), and it changes from moment to moment, moving between immediate perception of the environment, fantasy, and memories of the past hours and years earlier. The kinds of mental operation are various. So are the subjects that float into Stephen's mind, from theological problems to sex, from problems with his family and his writings to Irish history and politics. These subjects too assume protean forms, changing shape (the Fenian leader who escaped prison disguised as a bride), or changing nature (the host containing, or not containing, the real presence of Christ). Stephen thinks on the basis of experience, and carries out experiments with perception in order to do so. But his mind is also bookish: full of other people's words and conceptions which shape his thinking. His thought is shaped by Aristotle and by Berkeley, both philosophers important to Joyce, and an indicative combination of materialist and idealist, comparable to Joyce's own complementary pairing of Blake and Defoe (CW, 214), or to the many inconclusive confrontations between Shem and Shaun types throughout *Finnegans Wake*. Here they are seen primarily as having considered the relations of physical and mental reality in opposite ways. Aristotle asserted the material reality of the exterior world; Berkeley derived everything from his own mind, or, as Stephen thinks of it (both are treated with some humour), took 'the veil of the temple out of his shovel hat'. Stephen's mind is full too of poets, religious writers and theologians. Shakespeare and Blake, Boehme, Traherne and Swift, Arius and the Nicene Creed, William of Occam and Joachim da Fiore as well as the Bible, are all invoked in ways that help to define Joyce's theme or to characterise Stephen. As elsewhere, Stephen's learning has a vein of grotesque and scatological humour. Arius is remembered as much for his death in a watercloset as for his heresy on the relation of the Father and the Son. Nor is Stephen rich in reverence: Christ on the cross reminds him of his appointment with Mulligan in a pub ('I thirst'). Stephen's mind constantly moves to a humorous and irreverent view of whatever floats into it. It is of Stephen in Proteus that Joyce remarked to Frank Budgen, 'I haven't let this young man off very lightly, have I?'.[2] Stephen does not let himself off lightly either. It is not Stephen's least attractive quality that his irreverence is applied to himself – his Parisian affectations, his smutty sexual interests, his cowardice, even his writings. But unlike Mulligan, Stephen is not fixed in a stock response of humorous distancing: he can be serious too, as when he considers the sufferings of Irish history and identifies imaginatively with the sufferers: 'my people ... Their blood is in me' (38/45).

Telemachus and Nestor use interior monologue sparingly and with clear points of transition. Proteus is more radically experimental in the way it renders consciousness. Here Joyce moves frequently back and forth between objective narration and a much more varied interior monologue, with the two simply

juxtaposed. The reader thus sees both sides of Stephen's problem
– the world he is walking through and its impact on his mind
– and sometimes shares Stephen's doubt about which is which
when no point of view is clearly signalled. The interior
monologue moves between perception, fantasy and memory,
usually by some evident process of connection. Sometimes this
is verbal: the Sandymount Pigeonhouse reminds Stephen of his
life in Paris where he read Léo Taxil's irreligious *Vie de Jésus*
with its satire of the conception of Christ in which the
inseminating Holy Spirit is '*le pigeon*'. Sometimes the connection
is conceptual, as in the sequence: midwife, navel, link of the
generations, Adam and Eve, Stephen's parents, parents and
children, the Father and the Son (32/38). The most striking
experiments of this chapter are with language itself. Again, how
we perceive is the issue. The language Stephen has to see with
affects what he can see, as Stephen recognises when he tries out
words from different languages for the same action (40,392–3/47).
Joyce too, therefore, experiments with protean transformations
of language, by using foreign languages and special varieties of
English, by special arrangements of English bringing out its
musical qualities, by colourful invented compounds ('loudlatin-
laughing'), and by invented 'languages' given to the sea, the
wind, the planets. There are even glimpses of *Finnegans Wake*
('contransmagnificandjewbangtantiality'). It is a technical *tour
de force* of narrative method and linguistic invention that
prepares in brief for many of the later more extended
experiments.

II   ODYSSEY

4.   *Calypso (Odyssey, V)*

As Telemachus does for Stephen, Calypso lays the foundations
of Bloom's character: his relations with Molly, his feelings about
his children, his sexual interests, his practical and commercial

habits of mind, and his partly Jewish background. It is evident
from Bloom's pork breakfast that he is not orthodox. He never
has been: Bloom's father renounced Judaism the year before
Bloom was born. Nevertheless, Bloom's self-identity is in part
Jewish. Agendath Netaim, planters' company, *Bleibtreustrasse*
('remain-true street'), a scheme to establish a Zionist colony in
the Old Testament homelands, becomes one of the motifs of
his day. As well as 7 Eccles Street it is Odysseus–Bloom's Ithaca.
Complementary is Bloom's good-luck potato, the staple national
food without which there is famine, given to Bloom by his Irish
mother, and so symbolic of his Irishness. The first three Bloom
episodes correspond to the three of the Telemachia for Stephen,
showing their separate activities at the same times of the day
before their paths cross for the first time in Aeolus. Bloom and
Stephen are in many ways obviously different. They are even
held to exemplify opposite character types: 'The scientific. The
artistic' (558/683). But opposites in Joyce, like Shem and Shaun
in *Finnegans Wake*, also have about them a kind of identity,
are extremes that meet, or at least depend upon each other for
their definition, a view which Joyce enforced by reference to his
favourite philosopher–heretic, Giordano Bruno.[3] Though Bloom
is the scientific personality there is also 'a touch of the artist
about old Bloom' (193/235): he has tried his hand at a Joycean
preliminary to fiction (56, 519–20/69). The opposite identities
of Bloom and Stephen are capable of fusion or exchange:
Stoom, Blephen (558/682). Their tentative relationship is one
central issue of *Ulysses*, and from the beginning Joyce sets up
a pattern of correspondences between them, minor and major.
Like Stephen, Bloom has a *Hamlet* theory (15/17;62/76). The
same cloud covering the sun evokes in each a similar mood –
Stephen's personal, Bloom's racial.[4] Both are without keys,
symbolic of dispossession. In some echoes there is comic contrast
– as in their different *Hamlet* theories – but there is also
a thematic interest in the whole pattern related to the motif
'metempsychosis'. The separateness of individual identity is
questioned from within and from without. Stephen associates
imaginatively with an historical past ('I, a changeling' (38/45)),

though he feels disconnected from last-year's self ('Other fellow
did it: other me' (35/41)). Bloom and Stephen find their
experiences paralleled in people they meet (Stephen in Sargent
(23/27), Bloom in M'Coy (60/73)). As Bloom later has it, 'one
life is all' (230/280). The many Stephen/Bloom echoes, like the
basic technique of variations on Homeric myth, imply that he
is right.

The main variation on Homeric myth in this episode is played
by Molly. She is Calypso, 'the concealer' – of a message not, as
in Homer, for Odysseus, but for herself: Boylan's letter. Molly's
island home is Gibraltar, the Greek name for which – Calpe –
enforces her Homeric identity. Dlugacz, the middle-European
Jew and Zionist 'enthusiast', is Bloom's Hermes recalling him
to Zion/Ithaca. Just as Bloom and Stephen meet other selves
there is too another Calypso – the *Photo-Bits* nymph, not unlike
Molly (53/65) – and Molly herself has an alternative fictional
prototype. *Voglio et non vorrei* (the phrase is adapted from *Don
Giovanni*) shows Molly as a willing–reluctant Zerlina about to
be seduced by Don Blazes Boylan. At first Bloom is perplexed
about how to pronounce the fatal word, *voglio* ('I want to').
Later he becomes the Don's successful opponent, the avenging
Commendatore.

5. Lotus-Eaters (Odyssey, IX, 82–104)

The informing idea of Lotus-Eaters is escapism, sometimes
treated neutrally as ease or relaxation, sometimes with the
understated horror of paralysis which is a main theme of
Dubliners. There are many modes of evading the problems of
being fully human, not all as obvious as eating the tranquillising
lotus. Bloom is the principal lotus-eater, but Joyce as usual
reinforces his theme in narrative detail and style. Bloom's
epistolary affair with Martha Clifford is his main escape. There
may be 'no roses without thorns' (64/78), but Bloom throws
away Martha's pin. A rose without a thorn is what he is after,
and so he dwells on images of peaceful relaxation – a *dolce far*

niente vision of the East conjured up by the Oriental Tea Company, a 'long long long rest' fantasised on the basis of a painting of Mary and Martha. Bloom also enjoys various minor evasions: he will not think of Boylan's name, or of his father's suicide, indulges himself with the narcotic of a cigar, or imagines himself lapped in the 'womb of warmth' of his projected bath. Lotus-eating, however, is not only for Bloom, nor only for obvious hedonists and degenerates. Bloom sees evasion where it is least expected, in the hypnotised military – literally not a bit asleep, metaphorically thoroughly so. The conformity of a uniform, the orders of the drill-yard, take from them the burden of responsibility for their own decisions. Religion, 'opium of the people', is the drug Bloom dwells on most, and in his most amusing style: this drug is not for him. Buddhism and Christianity may look very different in their central images – passive acceptance, active suffering – but the effect of Christianity in Bloom's vision is not unlike the Buddhist lotus, 'joss-sticks burning': Christianity is a powerful opiate that 'stupefies ... lulls all pain'. Joyce does not dissociate himself from this, but the view is clearly presented with a Bloomish tinge. 'Punish me, please ... Lovely shame': in imagining confession and penance Bloom sees the delicious threats of punishment he has elicited in Martha's letter and will elicit again as James Lovebirch and in the sado-masochistic Bella episode of Circe.

The natural flower, perfume and drug associations of the lotus are worked into details throughout the episode: in Bloom's pseudonym and his 'language of flowers', in Martha's gift and her question ('What perfume ...?'), in Bloom's ruminations on the chemist's stock and the odour of lemon soap. The style reinforces the langorous, perfumed atmosphere, not only when Bloom directly imagines oriental torpor but even when he imagines Guinness (the domestic Irish lotus) flowerily flowing from a bunghole, 'winding through mudflats all over the level land, a lazy pooling swirl of liquor bearing along wideleaved flowers of its froth'. There is also, however, an opposite current, in the style and in Bloom himself. Joyce's unsignalled jumps between narrative, dialogue and interior monologue, recalling the past and abruptly switching to the present, have for the reader precisely the opposite effect to the lulling cadences of imagined oriental lethargy. Similarly, Bloom himself is wide awake, in his quick-thinking evasion of M'Coy's borrowing ploys, his lively anti-religious humour ('I.N.R.I.? ... Iron nails ran in' (66/81)), and his on-the-*qui-vive* alertness to taking pleasure in women – 'Watch! Watch! Silk flash rich stockings white. Watch!'. Bloom goes in for plenty of lotus-eating in the course of his day, but it is not the main thing about him.

6. *Hades (Odyssey, XI)*

Hades in a minor way prefigures Wandering Rocks in giving an extended view of Dublin. On the journey to Glasnevin cemetery, Brian Boroimhe (Boru) house, Nelson's Column, the statues of William Smith O'Brien and Daniel O'Connell, and the plinth of Parnell's statue (the statue itself was not erected until 1911) are reminders of a spectrum of Irish history, filled out by Bloom's graveyard thoughts of Robert Emmet. We hear more of Parnell and O'Connell in Glasnevin, where both are buried. Joyce also portrays the city by drawing in a number of characters from *Dubliners*. It is fiction referring to fiction, but, amongst so much realistic Dublin detail, the knowledge that these characters exist outside *Ulysses* heightens the feeling of reference to an actual world. The *Dubliners* characters bring with them *Dubliners* themes: emotional paralysis and religious factionalism. Catholic versus Protestant does not exhaust Dublin's religious excuses for conflict. Haines and Mr Deasy have already given voice to English and Ulster anti-Semitism. Joyce includes anti-Semitism here as also part of the Dublin Catholic ethos. He will return to it in Cyclops in the context of nationalism.

   Being Jewish, Bloom is an outsider to the Catholic ceremony he attends. His companions, on first-name terms with each other, think of Bloom and address him, as he thinks of and addresses them, by surname: Hynes does not know his first name; Menton pointedly ignores him. Bloom is isolated, but he is not unique. Hades brings him for the first time into conjunction with Boylan.

The trauma of the moment continues to echo later, but as Bloom thinks of the marriages of his companions it is evident that his problems are not unusual. Mrs Martin Cunningham's habitual drinking is her husband's stone of Sisyphus. Mr Power keeps a (Platonic) mistress ('You would imagine that would get played out pretty quick' is Bloom's verdict). The funeral itself is not that of an ideal husband: Paddy Dignam, like Homer's Elpenor, died of 'too much John Barleycorn'. Even Mr Dedalus's genuine grief for his wife seems a matter of fits and starts: moments before his collapse he is 'never better'. Bloom struggles with his marital problems alone, but they are typical.

As well as placing Bloom in his Dublin context, Hades develops the novel's parents and children preoccupation by crossing for the first time the paths of Stephen and Bloom. As Bloom watches Simon Dedalus react to Stephen, he reflects on fathers and sons, what his own dead son might have been, and the parallel relationship that is – that of his wife and daughter:

> Full of his son. He is right. Something to hand on. If little Rudy had lived ... My son. Me in his eyes ... Molly. Milly. Same thing watered down. (73–4/89)

'Something to hand on'. Queen Victoria too, Bloom reflects, had 'something new to hope for' in her son, but instead was c' 'essed with a dead past. As a son, Bloom too thinks of the past, the dead father, but not, like the old Queen, as a frozen attitude: he is naturally prompted by the funeral carriage discussion of suicide to think of his father's death, but his recollections are too precise, and his sense of comic possibilities too alert, for sentimentality. 'Gravediggers .. Shows the profound knowledge of the human heart' (90/109): Bloom's comment on the comedy of *Hamlet* identifies one of the great qualities of *Ulysses* itself.

Hades is saturated with death: the famous dead of Dublin; the dead remembered by each character individually; death and the animal world (the corpse-eating rat; the cattle going to slaughter); black and white as the colours of mourning; a vocabulary associated with mortality (Joyce enjoys some verbal play: 'gravely', 'dying out', 'dead against it', 'mortified'); and in the epic of the human body, the Hades organ (on which Joyce likewise punningly insists) is the pump of life and signifier of death, the heart. But though Bloom recognises fully its sorrows, he is not incapacitated by the thought of death: as in the novel as a whole, there is an assertion back towards life in Bloom's commonsensical comedy. The physical grotesqueness of decay in death and, even more than in Lotus-Eaters, the religious practices surrounding death, give rise to some of Joyce's funniest writing. Bloom's thoughts of the fertility of Glasnevin, embroidered by his commercial imagination ('Well preserved fat corpse, gentleman, epicure, invaluable for fruit garden'); his fantasies of preserving memories of the dead by means of the gramophone ('After dinner on a Sunday. Put on poor old greatgrandfather...kraark awfullygladaseeagain hellohello amawf krpthsth'); his vision of the Last Judgement ('every fellow mousing around for his liver and his lights and the rest of his traps'); and his adaptations of proverb and cliché ('The Irishman's house is his coffin') – these comic transformations of the funereal Joyce juxtaposes with genuine pathos.

7. Aeolus (Odyssey, X, 1–79)

Writing and language are the subjects of Aeolus – journalism, oratory, Stephen's writing, and Joyce's. Joyce explores the relationship between language, subject-matter, and consciousness, a typically Modernist concern, developed by the stylistic experiments of later episodes, that what we see depends on the language we have to see with. The journalistic headlines and picture-caption type headings are only the most obvious cases of how language conventions impose on, and even construct, the reality they ostensibly report. At times the pleasure to be had simply from Joyce's exuberant mastery of his styles is an end in itself, but there is also an underlying focus for the stylistic issue: Ireland, and the consequences of viewing her in different ways.

The chapter's styles of oratory, the Aristotelian divisions of epideictic (done for show), forensic (legal), and deliberative (political or hortatory), are exhibited by the reported speeches of Dan Dawson, Seymour Bushe, and John F. Taylor. Dawson and Taylor both give views of Ireland. Dawson's is romantic, 'Erin, green gem set in a silver sea'. An archaic, purely literary vocabulary makes no attempt to grasp a reality beyond language: it is designed to elicit a sentimental response to an artificial construction. Joyce comments by the counterpoint of some vivid vernacular exclamations, apparently from his father's conversation. 'High falutin stuff' is Bloom's verdict too, though he recognises that this rhetoric has a powerful appeal (and so evinces a common false consciousness, which is one ground of its importance). Seymour Bushe's style is more admired, though it too is compromised by archaism and cliché, and its obvious balanced parallels and cleverly reduplicated final clause make it an eloquence that draws attention to itself rather than to its subject. That subject, Moses, and Dawson's, Ireland, are brought together by John F. Taylor. Taylor parallels the Israelites enslaved by Egypt to the Irish under English domination. The Israelites' refusal of cultural domination and their eventual exodus and religious achievements are a moral for the Gaelic League's programme of reviving Irish culture and language. Joyce's attitude towards this is ambiguous. In itself the speech is much the most persuasive of the three examples of oratory. Joyce himself had used its imagery of Moses and the exodus with reference to Irish nationalism in writing of Parnell (*CW*, 225). It is the passage that Joyce chose for his own recording from *Ulysses*, in which he delivers the speech with great conviction. Stephen's response is divided. He resists its eloquence ('Noble words coming. Look out'), but he also succumbs to it. Taylor recalls for Stephen the greatest of all Irish political orators, Daniel O'Connell, to whom his response is likewise ambivalent: his words are both ephemeral, 'gone with the wind', and preserved in Akasic record (the infinite memory of nature). An adequate art – that is, one with a sufficiently comprehensive stylistic range – could also preserve the most ephemeral realities: Stephen's own writings are attempts at Akasic record, which is

a parallel to the epic comprehensiveness of *Ulysses* itself.
Stephen's overt response, however, is satire: his own realistic
and comic parable, a Pisgah vision of Ireland, the keynotes of
which are sexual frustration and the service of two masters:
Nelson, symbolic of English dominance; a chaotic vista of
churches, symbolic of the Roman. A nice detail from Bloom
aligns him with Stephen's satire: John F. Taylor's history, while
implying that it takes long views, takes short ones: 'out of the
house of bondage' is the approved account of the exodus, but
Bloom's comic mistaken reversal ('into . . . ') is nearer the truth.
If the Jews are a model for the Irish, the example of Bloom, the
roughly treated outsider, does not suggest that they are a hopeful
one.

  Competing visions of Ireland enter too into the temptations
for Stephen as a writer. His relations with the 'opal hush poets'
– that is, the mystical Yeats group – are not a problem, but he
is tempted by Taylor's rhetoric: 'Could you try your hand at
it yourself?' he asks. Even more tempting is editor Crawford's
suggestion of journalistic openings. Stephen is offered a partly
Joycean chance: 'Put us all into it . . . Father, Son and Holy
Ghost and Jakes M'Carthy' is a Ulyssean recipe; 'Something
with a bit of bite in it' – by which Crawford means with a
polemical message – is not. It has the 'savour of dogma – a
most proper thing in a priest but a most improper in a poet'
(*CW*, 100). Aeolus presents the extremes of Stephen's writing.
The Parable of the Plums, with its comic realism, is a *Dubliners*
style piece which Stephen is hardly confident enough to tell and
which it does not yet occur to him to write. The opposite pole
is the musically rhythmical speech of his verse, which he judges
a failure: the rhymes which should savour of youth, beauty and
colour are 'old men, penitent, leadenfooted, underdarkneath the
night'. Stephen is uncertain, but the chapter is a *tour de force*
for Joyce. Stuart Gilbert remarks that it might serve as a textbook
of rhetorical devices, and he reproduces a list with examples of
many of the chapter's rhetorical figures. There is great inventive
zest about these stylistic explorations, as there is about Joyce's
play with the vocabulary of winds (for Aeolus), and his

variations on the chapter's colour, red (for Aeolus/Crawford's irascibility). In this context 'Pen is champ' plays nicely with a name.

More *Dubliners* characters are brought into Aeolus. So too are historical figures – accessories to the Phoenix Park murders of 1882: Fitzharris, now keeper of the cabman's shelter, and Gumley, now a corporation night-watchman and friend of Mr Dedalus (503/616). Like *Dubliners*, Aeolus is full of disappointment and frustration. Moses sees but does not enter the homeland (the temporary fate of Ulysses himself as a result of the gift of Aeolus); Bloom fails to clinch his advertising deal; J. J. O'Molloy fails to fulfil his youthful promise, to get his loan, even to tell his story of Baron Palles. The Vestal Virgins of Stephen's parable also have only a 'Pisgah sight', and their story is full of hinted sexual frustration made explicit in their final headline. Failure to reach goals is epitomised by the emblematic paralysis – Joyce's crucial term from the first page of *Dubliners* – of the transport system, 'becalmed in short circuit'. 'If I can get to the heart of Dublin I can get to the heart of all the cities of the world', Joyce told Arthur Power (*JJ*, 505). Dublin and Dubliners, as the mythic correspondences imply, are everywhere. So it is too with Irish history and politics. The opposed temperaments of England and Ireland are a permanent human opposition: for professor MacHugh it is Rome against Greece. The Phoenix Park murders are part of the nightmare of specifically Irish history from which Stephen is trying to awake, but their typicality is confirmed by the latest news – the assassination in Finland of a Russian 'lord lieutenant', so-called: Joyce points the parallel with English rule in Ireland.

8. Lestrygonians (Odyssey, X, 80–134)

Lestrygonians is about eating. Some of the eating is metaphoric, for Bloom's state of feeling ('eaten and spewed'), or his vision of human competitiveness ('eat or be eaten'). Most is literal. *Ulysses* is the epic of the human body, and Joyce is no more above the mundane facts of the body's taking in food than of its expelling waste, a regard for the everyday which has Homeric precedent in the *Odyssey*'s detailed accounts of heroic ingestion. Lestrygonians offers descriptions of eating (a greasily repulsive *tour de force* evokes what disgusts Bloom in the Burton): Bloom's reflections on the artificially created tastes of the rich and malnutrition of the poor; on vegetarianism, for and against; and, inevitably (the Lestrygonians eat Odysseus's companions), on cannibalism. Like Glasnevin this provokes Bloom's irreligious humour, still with food in view: his lewd limerick on eating the missionary MacTrigger, and his sceptic's sense that the missionary's God too has a Lestrygonian aspect ('God wants blood victim' (124/151)).[5]

Lestrygonians emphasises Bloom's compassion – for the hungry gull he feeds, for the blind boy he helps, for Mrs Purefoy in her long labour. Bloom does not act out his 'eat or be eaten' vision. His sexual rival is a threat constantly evaded, in thought, and finally in fact. His 'eaten and spewed' emotional state derives from a contrasting of past and present. To make this comprehensible Lestrygonians fills in Bloom's past, with indicative incidents. A younger, more fiery Bloom, as quasi-socialist Home-Ruler, joins a demonstration against Liberal Unionist, Joseph Chamberlain.[6] Meeting his old flame, Josie Powell/Mrs Breen, draws into his thoughts various admirers of Molly. The connection is only apparently unconscious.[7] Bloom's great moment of recollection, which echoes throughout his day, is of kissing Molly on Ben Howth. It is framed by a grim contrast: trapped flies, stuck, buzzing to escape, symbolise Bloom's present state (144/176). Bloom's melancholy gives rise to a Hamlet-like meditation on the cyclical metamorphoses of food: 'food, chyle, blood, dung, earth, food'. Similar reflections on the larger cycles of birth and death in a context of aeons of human effort subject to decay lead to the gloomy conclusion, 'No one is anything'. But, 'poached eyes on ghost' (the spectre of Parnell seen in his brother); 'tinned salmon. Well tinned in there' (in the small house of the Provost of Trinity, the Reverend Dr Salmon): Bloom is never far from a reviving sense of the humorous, which Joyce, as always, wittily aligns with his theme.

'Peristaltic' is Joyce's account of the Lestrygonian style – that is, forcing along by waves of contraction, as the alimentary canal moves food in the body. If one looks at Lestrygonians in terms of this idea there is something to see, in subject matter (Bloom's fantasy of watching digestion through the newly discovered X-rays), and in the way the narrative progresses (Bloom's movements, pausing before various eating houses, prompted onwards by goadings of body and mind – hunger; and at the Burton, disgust; and throughout, a dread of meeting Boylan). This may be a view of the Lestrygonian manner which, without Joyce's help, the novel would not of itself suggest to the most fit reader, but the style operates at more obvious levels than the peristaltic. 'Too much fat on the parsnips' (unctuous Davy Byrne); 'plovers on toast' (Nosey Flynn on Molly's pampered life-style); 'he couldn't swallow it all' (King Cormac Mac Art, incomplete – and ahistorical – convert to Christianity). The charms of Joyce's food-coloured vocabulary keep the eating theme in view.

9. *Scylla and Charybdis (Odyssey, XII, 1–259)*

Before Wandering Rocks gives a cross-section of Dublin, Scylla and Charybdis, set in the National Library, shows Dublin literary society, the world of the Irish Literary Renaissance. Temporarily Stephen is Odysseus; the Irish Renaissance group are his Charybdis. Their interest in Platonism, Theosophy and the transcendental, Stephen mocks and rejects – though his quotations from Shelley and Blake show that there is a part of his mind, here in abeyance, to which this appeals. In the present context the group's power of patronage is a stronger lure, and from that Stephen has no need to exclude himself (158/192). Aristotle is Stephen's Scylla, not in himself to be avoided (Odysseus is to sail nearer the rock as the less dangerous route): Plato's schoolboy is a weapon against his master. But this weapon can make Stephen a mocker and encourage him in the Mulliganesque. This is the true Scyllan danger. Attractive and amusing though Mulligan is, he is also coarse and brutal, given to taking always the lowest view. Earlier Stephen sees him as a betrayer. Here Judas and the accusers of Socrates reiterate the betrayal theme. It is at the crucial moment of his first encounter with Bloom that Stephen decides he and Mulligan must separate.

Stephen's Shakespeare theory is the main issue of Scylla and Charybdis. The theory needs to be seen in the context of what it opposes. It characterises Stephen as iconoclastic, opposite to orthodoxies about *Hamlet* (the Goethean 'hesitating soul ... torn by conflicting doubts'; for Stephen 'Khaki Hamlets don't hesitate to shoot'), opposite to orthodoxies about literature more generally. Stephen's antidote to bardolatry is his portrait of Shakespeare the unscrupulous time-server. Stephen will have nothing of A. E.'s view that Shakespeare's plays can be disconnected from his life. He insists on biography as an antidote to A. E.'s art-for-art's-sake nineties aestheticism ('As for living, our servants can do that for us'), but behind that conflict lies a more fundamental one: Stephen rejects A. E.'s Platonist view of art as revealing 'formless spiritual essences'. Against this, Stephen is a Joycean realist invoking Augustine: 'hold to the now, the here, through which all future plunges to the past'. The Shakespeare theory characterises Stephen, but it has many other functions. A theory about the presence of the artist in his work meaning, as Stephen finally concedes, that in *Hamlet* Shakespeare is both Ghost and Prince, the theory hints, if we apply it to *Ulysses*, that Joyce is present as much in Bloom as in the declared 'portrait of the artist'. It also bears on the issue central to *Ulysses* of fathers and sons, physical and spiritual – on Stephen's relationship with Simon Dedalus and Bloom's with Rudy; on Bloom's relations with Stephen, and even Stephen's with Ireland: Shakespeare is 'the father of all his race'; he has played a part in forming England's consciousness of itself, as Stephen wishes to do for Ireland. The Irish national epic, which in 1904 is 'yet to be written' (158/192), is the book we are reading. Like Shakespeare's plays it will forge the uncreated conscience of the race – a matter on which Stephen quotes Joyce (*P*, 253; *Letters*, II, 311). Unknown to Stephen, Shakespeare in his theory is also parallel to Bloom. Shakespeare is Odysseus

(wounded, like his own Adonis, by the boar's tusk (161/196));
Ann Hathaway is his adulterous anti-Penelope. Like Ann
Hathaway, Molly was the knowing wooer (157/191;612/743).
Hamnet Shakespeare is the dead son whom the playwright must
replace by a 'son of his soul' – his work (for Bloom the surrogate
son will be Stephen). But beyond the particular analogies the
cases are not peculiar. The father–son complications of Shakespeare's relation to *Hamlet* are analogous to the Trinitarian
mystery of the Father and the Son, which is itself the archetype
of all fatherhood and sonship. Stephen's theory wrestles with
a basic problem of father–son separation and identity. Stephen's
rejection of physical fathers is consequent on his own emotional
needs. Stephen does not recognise this himself, but Joyce implies
it by having Stephen recognise a parallel evasion in Eglinton.
As Stephen embarks on rejecting the importance of physical
fatherhood, he reflects that Eglinton ignores Shakespeare's
biography because he wishes to deny his father. This evokes in
Stephen a crucial memory marking his own distance from Simon
Dedalus. It is Joyce's hint to the reader: we should draw a
conclusion parallel to Stephen's on Eglinton. Joyce's character
is a son only. As a father himself Joyce thought fatherhood the
most important experience a man could have (*JJ*, 204).

Stephen treats his Shakespeare theory with passion, humour
and scepticism. We know from Telemachus that the theory is
a favourite topic long-brooded, and it seems that Joyce himself
described a similar theory in his (lost) lectures on *Hamlet* given
in Trieste in 1912–13. Stephen's self-scepticism is evident. He
declares it, and the account is constantly interrupted by his
self-ironic thoughts. But there is not in *Ulysses*, as there had
been in *Stephen Hero* and *A Portrait*, any play of irony around
Stephen's irony about himself. On the contrary, in Scylla and
Charybdis Joyce presents sympathetically Stephen's high
aspirations and his feelings of isolation from the Dublin literati.
Asked about his mythological name, Stephen reflects with
self-deflation: 'hawklike man. You flew. Whereto? Newhaven
–Dieppe, steerage passenger. Paris and back. Lapwing. Icarus.
Pater, ait. Seabedabbled, fallen, weltering'. He is not now

Daedalus but Icarus calling for his father as he falls into the sea. But at the climactic moment of the narrative, as Stephen encounters Bloom for the first time and simultaneously decides to separate from Mulligan, Stephen remembers a new element of his previous night's dream: 'last night I flew. Easily flew. Men wondered'. The only contextual comment is the meeting with Bloom, which the dream prophesied correctly. In treating Stephen as both Daedalus and Icarus, Joyce shows him as the Shakespeare-type artist, 'himself his own father'.

The narrative voice of Scylla and Charybdis does not come from a point of view which is critically placed, its attitudes are not elsewhere in the novel discredited, and so the reader naturally associates it with Joyce. It is important, therefore, in this most evidently autobiographical episode, that the narrative voice shares attitudes and stylistic features with Stephen: his mockery of the Dublin mystical literati (which the narrative voice conveys by its mannered ornateness in dealing with the group), his constant Shakespearean allusion, and his delight in playfully exploring names. This is sometimes just a matter of local humour: in Nell Gwynn Herpyllis Joyce combines Aristotle and Charles II, philosopher and Merry Monarch, via sex and death-bed bequests; Stephen's 'Lawn Tennyson' is the essence of upper-class Englishness. But the play with names is also thematic. Names are central to Stephen's Shakespeare theory, and to his and Joyce's explorations of the nature of individual identity. Others before Joyce have played meaningfully with names, as Shakespeare did with his own name in the sonnets and as Wilde did in understanding the sonnets (W. H., Willie Hughes, hews, hues). Two characters in Scylla and Charybdis, A. E. (George Russell) and John Eglinton (W. K. Magee), are what others have been ('Mr Sidney Lee, or Mr Simon Lazarus', 'rutlandbaconsouthamptonshakespeare'): mummers in names. Joyce and Stephen continue the mumming, with them, and with Best and Mulligan, as Joyce himself did outside the novel. Stephen's Shakespeare theory, connecting the writer's life with the names in his fictions, invites the reader to recall that 'Stephen Daedalus' was Joyce's own pseudonym for the *Dubliners* stories published in Russell's *The Homestead* in 1904. 'What's in a name?', asks Mageeglinjohn, giving an answer by the very act of choosing a pseudonym. That in itself indicates that names have meanings – in art ('Marina ... a child of storm, Miranda, a wonder, Perdita, that which was lost'), and in life (Stephen, *stephanos*, a crown; A. E., from aeon, suited to Russell, theosophist). Joyce draws out these meanings, or suggests appropriate meanings in the mummery of new names – auric egg; auk's egg (Stephen mocks Russell's theosophy); Stephen Dedalus, S. D. – Stephen, A. E.-style, but also suggesting to him *sua donna* (Stephen mocks himself through his own pre-occupation with his lack of a sexual partner). Mulligan is Puck Mulligan as mischievous mocker, Cuck Mulligan as specifically mocker of cuckolds, pseudo Malachi as false prophet, Ballocky Mulligan as indecent author. Obvious qualities of Eglinton are suggested by Judge Eglinton, Steadfast John, John sturdy Eglinton, ugling Eglinton. Chin Chon Eg Lin Ton is Puck Mulligan mockery. Ugling is Besteglinton when his opinion keeps the Irish Renaissance roadway; and Eclecticon when he has no opinion but what he has gathered from others: the collapse of his name mums the lack of authentic individuality in his thought. Joyce shows the reader how to unpack these playful names, *Finnegans Wake* style, with Molly's account of Ben Dollard, base barreltone (126/154). The reader who does as well as Molly will find 'it all works out'.

10. *Wandering Rocks (Odyssey, XII, 59–72)*

Wandering Rocks has the slightest Homeric source of all the episodes of *Ulysses*. Circe tells Odysseus of the two rocks, the Symplegades, in the Bosphorus between the coasts of Europe and Asia, which crash together destroying any ship that passes between them. Odysseus declines the route in favour of Scylla and Charybdis. Joyce's episode consists of eighteen short sections and a coda. The fragments are overlapping not sequential in time, and the first and last, which act as a frame, show church and state: journeys through Dublin of Father

Conmee and the Lord Lieutenant of Ireland. The sections are linked: almost all contain one or more brief and sometimes inscrutable intrusions from another. Some of these merely indicate simultaneity in time. Some are more pointed, as when Bloom and Boylan are brought together, both buying gifts for Molly, both finding incidental sexual gratification for themselves. The journeys of Father Conmee and the Lord Lieutenant intrude most, acting as a linking thread which emphasises their church-and-state thematic importance. The episode characterises Dublin as a place (Joyce's realism is here at its most detailed), as a living community, and through its history, which is drawn in tangentially.

In the Linati schema Joyce calls Dublin here 'the *hostile* environment': the hostilities are various. Joyce recalls the revolution of 1798 and its aftermath through its songs – 'The Memory of the Dead', 'The Croppy Boy' – and its famous victims – Tone, Emmet, Edward Fitzgerald. He goes back to Tudor conflicts – Gerald Fitzgerald versus the church; his grandson, Silken Thomas, versus the state – and comes forward to the current nationalist debate about use of the Irish language (the debate is 'Hell opened to Christians'). The hostility of the Irish environment to English rule is made clear by a rare piece of fictional geography: the river Poddle, which does not actually run on the Lord Lieutenant's route, is moved in order to hang out 'in fealty a tongue of liquid sewage' (207/252). But the environment is not only hostile. There is poverty (the begging war-wounded sailor; the Dedalus home), but there is also generosity (Molly and Bloom are united as generous givers – to the sailor, to the Dignam family fund); there is anti-Semitism and mockery of Bloom, but also a just acknowledgement of his virtues. The bad is balanced by the good – by the decency of Martin Cunningham (organising the Dignam fund), and the heroism of Tom Rochford (in his reported sewer rescue). Religion, in the person of Father Conmee, is depicted ambiguously. Father Conmee may be taken at face value as a kindly old man. The portrait can also be seen as satiric. Smiling to show his carefully cleaned teeth, Father Conmee is perhaps a touch too self-conscious in his ingratiating manners to 'important' people. Though convinced of the 'invincible ignorance' of Protestants he is not rigorous in his own theology: he accepts the 'reasonable plea' that being baptised a Catholic is not necessary for salvation, and that extreme unction is not a necessary rite. On one view these are humane beliefs. On another they are comfortable evasions lacking the rigour which Joyce, despite his loss of faith, continued to admire in Catholic theology.

Stephen is the person most in danger from hostile wandering rocks, 'between two roaring worlds where they swirl'. The roaring worlds that threaten him are those of the outer and the inner life, the second part creation of the first.[8] Lucifer's defiant *non serviam*, and the oblique defiance of exile, silence and cunning, were Stephen's alternative attitudes in *A Portrait*. The choice here is similar. The unabashed Stephen defies God in Buck Mulligan vein: he is 'bawd and butcher' – bawd to the Holy Ghost with the Blessed Virgin, butcher of the Son, '*dio boia*, hangman God' (175/213). Offering himself as Hamlet to God's Polonius, Stephen also propitiates him (199/242): the Paley watchmaker analogy gives appropriate praise – the universe is a wonderful mechanism. Stephen evades the wandering rock of religion only to run into that of his family, his sister Dilly 'drowning' in poverty. To help her would be to drown in her problems. Leaving her to drown provokes that guilt which he feels above all as a result of his comparable self-preservation in the face of his dying mother's need.

Wandering Rocks is a miniature *Dubliners* in subject and mode, with radiant realistic detail epitomising some aspect of city or citizens. Master Dignam exhibits the method at its most eloquent. His impatience with adult ways of mourning in which he cannot share; his vanity about his special status as a mourner; his casual thought of violence between parents and children – how his friend Stoer's 'old fellow welted hell out of him'; his boyish enthusiasm, entirely forgetting his father's death, for a boxing match; but then suddenly arising out of all this his vividly specific memories connected with the death: the sound of screws when the coffin was closed, his father drunk and going out to get more drunk, his father's last words. Joyce unsentimentally juxtaposes the most mundane and the deepest feeling, and precisely catches the vocabulary and shape of phrase of each for the individual character. Critics who displace attention from the particular to the variation on a theme (parents and children), or who persuade themselves that technique here, brilliant as it is, is other than the semi-transparent vehicle of human content, do Joyce no service.

11.   Sirens (*Odyssey, XII, 36–200*)

Sirens explores the obvious issue of its Homeric source, the relationship of music and sex. With his exposition of Stephen, Bloom and Dublin accomplished, Joyce begins in Sirens the radical experiments with style which in *Ulysses* culminate with Circe, and in his work as a whole with *Finnegans Wake*. The musical arrangements of language in Sirens, the play with, distortion and formation of words, make this the episode of *Ulysses* most akin to the *Wake*. Joyce invents and exploits a music of language which helps him to explore the Sirens-music-sex subject. Musical Ireland is also part of Joyce's subject. The episode's range of composers and musical styles, the musical knowledge and ability of ordinary patrons of the hotel bar, and the enthusiasm for music of all present characterise Ireland, as the same qualities did at the Misses Morkans' party in 'The Dead'.

The episode's primary sirens are the Ormond barmaids who, from behind 'their reef of counter', titillate the exclusively male clientèle. They are sirens to all men, not particularly to Odysseus –Bloom (though Bloom is specifically Odysseus tied to the mast, kept in his place by the pressure of Boylan's presence, and humorously 'gyved' by the elastic band he fiddles with in his pocket). Neither barmaid sings, but as Bloom says, 'there's music everywhere': Miss Douce's '*sonnez la cloche*' routine is her siren song. Other women too, as they appear in the episode, are presented as sirens: Martha by association with a song of unsatisfied yearning from an opera bearing her name; Molly as Bloom first met her, 'throat warbling ... Luring. Ah, alluring'; and the whore of the lane, a would-be but failed siren. Bloom's previous encounter with her is recalled by an ironic invocation of the *Martha* aria, 'When first he saw that form endearing'.

Bloom's feelings are the main human substance of the episode. He is upset by the presence of Boylan as the hour of his assignation with Molly approaches, but, though moved by both the love-song and the political ballad, 'The Croppy Boy', Bloom also maintains a degree of detachment. Like the croppy, with whose ballad the articulation of Bloom's feelings is entwined and by which his feelings are partly shaped, Bloom bears no hate. He sees deeper than the commonplace passions of jealously: 'Hate. Love Those are names. Rudy. Soon I am old'. Children; death; living your life; these are what is important. Even more readily is Bloom detached from the political sentiments which the ballad excites in others: he exits early, with strictures on music's effect of total emotional absorption ('thinking strictly prohibited'); untouched by reverence for any sacred cows of nationalism, he farts while reading the famous last words of Robert Emmet.

Bloom's feelings apart, music is the main focus of Joyce's lavish inventiveness throughout the episode – what language can do to describe effects of music, but more especially all the means by which language can itself be music. Joyce's schema describes the episode as written in a musical form, *fuga per canonem*, and Stuart Gilbert shows how the episode can be analysed in these terms. The Sirens' song is the fugal subject; Bloom's entry and monologue is the answer; Boylan is the countersubject; the episodes work these in together, often overlapping them with abrupt unmarked cutting from one element to another, between paragraphs and even within sentences. Gilbert's musical analysis is ingenious, but it is the kind of thing that no reader (however familiar with fugal technique) would perceive without being told it. More clearly part of the episode's effectiveness are Joyce's experiments with the music of language. This is partly a matter of the arrangement of words for musical effect, using all the traditional devices of alliteration, assonance, onomatopoeia, patterned structure, rhythm and rhyme, though with many very untraditional dislocations of grammar and word order. Much of the episode's stylistic experimentation is of this kind, but there is also more radical experimentation with semantic content, form and sound. Joyce's word play, for example, is not straightforward, as when 'jingle' is used as both verb and noun, as a Boylan motif suggesting his brash confidence ('jaunty' is its constant companion), and to foreshadow the rattling of the Blooms' old bed as Boylan and Molly have sex. And when words which have a musical meaning – trio, fifth, quaver, descant, subject, answer, organ, concert (as a verb), even (more remotely) crotchety – are used in only their non-musical sense: some feeling of a pun is induced by the overall context of musical reference. The deformation of names illustrates most readily Joyce's play with form and sound. Bloowho, Bloowhose, Bloohimwhom, Greasabloom, Bloo, Seabloom; Kennygiggles, Bronzedouce; Lid, De, Cow, Ker, Doll: 'Essex bridge ... Yes ... Yessex'; 'Joe Maas ... Choirboy style ... Massboy'; Blazure: these have no single explanation. Mr Dedalus and his musical companions are a version of the tonic sol-fa. The renaming of Essex Bridge suggests Bloom assenting to one of his constant preoccupations. 'Blazure' is azure-eyed Blazes in his sky-blue bow. The play with Boylan's name seems at times a kind of mockery ('Too slow for Boylan, blazes Boylan, impatience Boylan, jogged the mare'), particularly since 'Boylan with impatience', taken over from Tom Rochford's joke in Wandering Rocks (191/232), is repeated here as an essence-of-Boylan motif. The disintegration of Bloom's name is more thematic, implying met him pike hoses/metempsychosis, questioning the solidity and separateness of individual identity. 'One life is all' Bloom reflects, as (unknowingly) he echoes Stephen's thought (230/280; 166/202). 'Siopold' shows him (Leopold) identified with Simon (to whom he listens) and with Lionel (whose song Simon sings):

Up the quay went Lionelleopold, naughty Henry with letter for
Mady, with sweets of sin with frillies for Raoul with met him
pike hoses went Poldy on. (236/288)

This highlights the issue of shifting identities and adds more
Bloom *personae*: Molly's Poldy, Martha's Henry, identifies with
the *Sweets of Sin* husband, financing adultery.

The characters too play with language. When Miss Kennedy
takes up Miss Douce's 'his ex' (excellency) with 'exquisite
contrast' the narrator elaborates: 'in exquisite contrast',
'inexquisite contrast, contrast inexquisite nonexquisite'. The
characters make language strange, as in Lenehan's mock reading
lesson, 'Ah fox met ah stork'; they transform words into
expressive sounds, as in Pat the waiter's haughtily sniffing
mockery, 'imperthnthn thnthnthn'; and they too pun, as in
Bloom's unintentional 'How will you pun? You punish me?',
or Simon Dedalus's thoroughly intentional innuendo about the
Blooms' secondhand clothes business, 'Mrs Marion Bloom has
left off clothes of all descriptions'. Some of this verbal play may
seem to endorse a Derridean view of the instability of language,
that language is a system of differences with no positive terms,
and non-referential because meaning is never finally reached by
closure. But when Joyce juxtaposes 'sloe' and 'slow' he seems
more concerned to show how readily we recognise, by context,
that the same sound has different senses; when he juxtaposes
'flowed' and 'flower' he shows how conclusive the differen-
tiating final letter is. Meaning is precisely not deferred: it is
clinched. Difference cannot be that vital to signification if 'tip',
'tep', 'tap', 'top' and 'tup' can all manage (as they do (226/274))
to mean 'fuck'.

12. Cyclops (Odyssey, IX)

In Sirens, Bloom's state of feeling is a main focus. In Cyclops,
the treatment of Bloom is exterior. There is no interior
monologue, which means that Joyce can maintain a comic tone
for the most painful moment of Bloom's day (Molly and Boylan
are now in bed together), a tone which is essential to Joyce's

urbane though none the less devastating satire of Irish nationalist
fanaticism. But despite the objective treatment our sympathies
remain with Bloom. He is grossly and wilfully misunderstood:
attacked by spongers for meanness when his errand is one of
practical generosity, by the violently intolerant because he argues
for toleration, and by racists because he is a Jew. His feelings
are allowed to peep through the exterior presentation in his
Freudian slip, 'the wife's admirers' for 'the wife's advisers'
(Boylan in mind); and in his passionate denunciation of how
his race is 'at this very moment, this very instant' robbed and
insulted – in Morocco. Bloom's political passion is wholly valid,
but it is also out of character with his usual prudent reserve.
Morocco (which played no special role in enslaving the Jews)
gives the key: exotic North Africa Bloom constantly associates
with Molly.

In Cyclops we see through two glasses, parody and an
anonymous narrator. The two styles – both equally (like the
Cyclops) one-eyed – mean an alternation of inflation and
sentimentality with belittlement and cynicism. The anonymous
narrator is aggressive in his attitude to everybody: the central
figure, the nationalist citizen, is 'all wind and piss like a tanyard
cat'; Jews are 'the bottlenosed fraternity'; Bloom is, 'old
lardyface ... old cod's eye'. But in spite of his violent attitudes
the narrator is not disgusting: his lively expression is too amusing
for that. His is a vernacular equivalent of the more literary use
of cliché of the Eumaeus narrator, which, even more than the
Eumaeus narrator, he varies in humorous ways. Cyclops is the
first of three episodes using parody, though the parodies here
are broader and less specific than in Nausikaa and Oxen of the
Sun. The Cyclops parodies interrupt the fiction grotesquely to
inflate some aspect of it, though Joyce also includes one parody
within the fiction (a piece, purportedly from the *United Irishman*,
on the visit to England of a Zulu chief). The similarity in subject
and tone between this satire of British imperialist racism and
the parodic interruptions goes some way to integrate the
extraordinary technique. It also implies an unholy alliance:
British imperialism/Irish nationalism – racism. In Cyclops, as

in the two following sections, the reader needs to recognise roughly the style that is being parodied (in Cyclops the broadness of the parodies means that this is no very sophisticated operation) and enjoy Joyce's inventiveness within the given style – his inflation of its mannerisms and the dissonances introduced for comic effect, as in the list of Irish heroes. This comedy of nationalist bigotry and ignorance includes Patrick W. Shakespeare and Brian Confucius (there's nothing good but it's Irish), alongside the genuinely Irish but inveterately anti-nationalist first Duke of Wellington, Arthur Wellesley (in *Finnegans Wake* Joyce makes great play with the duke's disclaimer of his Irishness by birth: 'If a gentleman happens to be born in a stable it does not follow that he should be called a horse'). The two main styles parodied are various journalistic modes and the kind of romantic re-writing of Irish myth and legend undertaken within the Yeats group, particularly by Lady Gregory (Stephen has slated her 'drivel' (177/216); Joyce reviewed her work unfavourably (CW, 102–5)). The journalistic parodies often work by means of an exuberantly grotesque disjunction between mode and subject, as in feature story (execution of an Irish patriot), theatrical puff (the citizen's dog humanised as Celtic bard), report of a society wedding (all the participants have tree names: subject, the re-afforestation of Ireland), and a *Church News* style account of a religious ceremony: all the loafers in the bar are canonised; the bar itself is consecrated as Dublin's Catholic cathedral (the two existing cathedrals are Church of Ireland). In their matter the journalistic parodies continue the satire of nationalism which the other main parodic mode embodies in its manner. Not all the parodies, however, are anti-nationalist: in two at least Bloom is the object of the comedy (257/313; 283/345). Much of the parody works in a general way, affecting tone and guiding attitude, but as usual with Joyce detail is often significant too. The Keogh–Bennett boxing match epitomises the English–Irish conflict, but it also implies more specific parallels. Like Keogh, Stephen fights a soldier. Like Keogh, a lamb whose blood is wine, Bloom is several times in Cyclops humorously Christ-like. The parallels identify Stephen and Bloom. Bennett is, like Polyphemus, (almost) one-eyed. This is appropriate for the Keogh/Bloom parallel, but ironic in that it identifies British soldier and Irish nationalist (the citizen too is Polyphemus). The ironic identity endorses Bloom's (and Joyce's) point throughout the episode: force is force, whether Irish or British.

The main representative of Irish nationalism in Cyclops is the citizen. Like the narrative modes, he is Polyphemus, mentally monocular, a fanatic; also a bar-room sponger whose corrupt practice is not consistent with his corrupt profession: he has taken over the land of an evicted tenant. Joyce attacks the rhetoric of nationalism and the claims it makes for ancient Irish culture, but especially he exposes its racism. Joyce is rarely an evidently political writer, but his account of nationalism here is prescient. The episode articulates a whole group of Hitlerian issues. The bar-loafers are xenophobic: the French are 'a set of dancing masters'; Germans are 'sausageeating bastards'. The citizen apparently has some notion of racial purity which leads him to spit at Bloom's claim to be Irish because he was born in Ireland. (Joyce liked to point out that any racial criterion of Irishness excluded most of the heroes of nationalist history including Tone, Emmet, Fitzgerald, and Parnell (*CW*, 161–2)). The nationalists encourage militaristic sports, and, associated with these, narrow notions of manliness in support of which they police dissent with slurs of effeminacy and homosexuality: Bloom is 'one of those mixed middlings'. As a Jew he is the archetypal, always available scapegoat.

To all this Bloom gives a serious answer. Injustice is wrong; force and hatred perpetuate it; love is central to a properly human life. Joyce does not mean to discredit this, but his own response to fanaticism is comedy, which he allows to play on all sides. Bloom, apparently unconscious of its national and class associations, recommends to admirers of hurley and putting the stone the shoneen game of lawn tennis: it is as comic as anything in the episode. And Joyce's whole presentation of nationalism, while he satirises unsparingly what is bad in it, is as two-eyed as it is urbane. Nationalist extremism is given some justification by the way in which Irish issues are dealt with by the British parliament, and nationalism is not isolated in its gross failings. Joyce pointedly includes examples of hideous cruelty based on racism, by England and Belgium in Africa, by England in India and by white America in its treatment of American blacks. To his credit the citizen does not rewrite history: albeit without Stephen's (and Joyce's) vehemence, he acknowledges Ireland's self-betrayal. Joyce endorses the citizen's attack on brutal authority and slavish quiescence in the British navy with his parody of the Apostles' Creed. The citizen's basic political argument too, on English economic warfare against Ireland, and on the depopulation caused by English malpractice and neglect, is sound. Bloom agrees. The arguments are Joyce's own (CW, 153–74).

13. Nausikaa (Odyssey, VI)

Nausikaa expands the presentation of love and sexual feeling in *Ulysses*. With Howth peninsula in the background (site of an often-recalled kiss), with his watch stopped at half past four (the hour of adulterous conjunction), Bloom thinks about himself and Molly as they were and as they have become. Masturbating in response to the titillations of Gerty MacDowell is his immediate way of coping. Masturbating releases emotional stress. Flirting with Gerty, *jeune fille en fleur*, is a relief from the complications of love and sex in middle age. The episode has a Homeric basis, but it has too, more than any other episode relating to Bloom, bases in Joyce's own life – in his relationships with Amalia Popper and Martha Fleischmann. Amalia Popper was a pupil of Joyce's in Trieste. Joyce knew her between 1907 and 1909. *Giacomo Joyce*, written in its final form probably in 1914 (that is, between *A Portrait* and *Ulysses*), is based principally on this relationship. There is some fictional rearrangement introducing material that can be dated between 1911 and 1914 (by which time Joyce was, like Bloom, in his thirties), though in other ways the piece is barely fictionalised. The middle-aged protagonist is called Jamesy and Jim; his wife is Nora. The young woman is Jewish, and, as with Bloom, her

race is important. The work's *Ulysses*-like mixture of sentiment
and irony expresses what Richard Ellmann calls 'the power of
love even as it attests the melancholy of human attempts to
enjoy it'.[9] Joyce's brief relationship with Martha Fleischmann
in 1918 and 1919 brings us yet nearer to *Ulysses*, Bloom and
Gerty MacDowell.[10] Martha was nearly Joyce's own age, but
Joyce was at first struck by her resemblance to the girl behind
Stephen's vision on the beach in *A Portrait*. He supposed initially
that (like Amalia Popper) she was Jewish. Joyce wrote to her
in a vein of extreme sentiment, though apparently also, in the
manner of Bloom with his Martha, trying out an expression
which this Martha considered indelicate. The correspondence
included a postcard addressed to Nausikaa from Odysseus
(*Letters*, II, 430, 428). Both relationships indicate how variously,
not only in Stephen, Joyce transformed his life into fiction, and
also, particularly in the experience articulated in *Giacomo Joyce*,
how Joyce saw in Homer's Nausikaa episode the germ of an
archetypal experience. Youth and innocence can reawaken for
middle age the possibility of wonder in love uncontaminated
by all the contingencies of marriage. Joyce is far from purely
romantic about such spiritual fireworks, but he allows their
validity within limits,

Innocence is, of course, relative. The innocence of a teenager
is not that of a child. Gerty MacDowell's lameness is symbolic.
Her sense of love and sex is powerfully coloured by the
sentimental romantic fiction she reads; whence the style of her
part of the episode. It is a style of stereotype in emotional ideal
– strong quiet manly men, matinée idols, and dreamhusbands –
and cliché in language. The cliché pretends that life is easier
than *Ulysses* shows it to be: problems are simply solvable, pains
easily assuaged. But there is a naïveté which is in its way innocent
about the completeness with which Gerty accepts her ruinous
myths. Joyce's parodic comedy is constantly mixed with pathos.
The social and emotional aspirations Gerty has been given by
her reading and by her subjection to the dictates of fashion
contrast pitifully with her actual life: her lameness, her father
who drinks and beats her mother, her 'love' for a boy who

kissed her when both were children (his family is Protestant, and, with a son at Trinity College, quite outside the social orbit of anyone whose grandpa lends his dog to the citizen). Religion, too, is implicated in Gerty's emotional vitiation. The juxtaposed service to the Virgin shows how in this form Christianity too is amenable to the style, and thence the vision, of the sentimental novelette. False consciousness such as Gerty's is able to feed off the sexual sublimations of Catholic myth, dogma and ritual. Stephen himself had once amply fed there, as did the young Joyce.[11] To Stephen now the Madonna is a figure which 'the cunning Italian intellect flung to the mob of Europe' (170/207): Mariolatry – veneration of the pure mother, woman without sexual 'stain' – makes good the lack of any focus for male sexuality in Christian myth. Mary is Athene, but with no complementary Aphrodite. Bloom sees the celibacy of priests as comparable in its function for women – 'tree of forbidden priest': their chastity too is sexually alluring. So Gerty finds it with Father Conroy.

Gerty's experience is, in a sense, easily broad enough to explode the clichés in terms of which she thinks and feels, but the control of language over experience is so powerful that Gerty remains the victim of her given fictions. She knows and does not know. Able to recognise that Bloom is masturbating and to encourage him in doing so, she still presents to herself an idealised account of him and of her own involvement in what he is doing. The language Gerty has been given actively prevents her from seeing her experience. Unable to name what she knows, in an important sense she cannot know it. Embarrassed by the word 'bottom', she cannot mention menstruation, intercourse, masturbation, even a toilet, except as 'that thing', 'that other thing', 'something not very nice', 'that place'. Nausikaa gives one answer to the charge that *Ulysses* is immoral in its sexual frankness: it is not fiction that shows things as they are, using the languages of experience, that causes emotional and moral damage. It is the argument Joyce put to Grant Richards in defending *Dubliners* as a moral, because truth-telling, fiction (*Letters*, II, 132–44).

Bloom's encounter with Gerty gives rise to a medley of sexual memories, speculations and fantasies. These are punctured by thoughts of advertising, but they rise too to a stoic nobility in reflections on ageing, transience and recurrence. Bloom's masturbation we can view neutrally. It is an ordinary matter. It is evident from Joyce's letters to Nora of December 1909 (*SL*, 180–92) that Joyce found the most frankly physical attitude to sex compatible with a refined spirituality in love. His attitude to masturbation has about it nothing of the sexual puritan. Molly masturbates (610/740; 634/771), as do the vestal virgins of Stephen's 'Parable of the Plums' – 'yet can you blame them?' (123/150). The one voice to condemn Bloom for masturbating is that of the anti-Semitic Junius in Oxen of the Sun (334/409). It is a voice of evidently nonsensical prejudices. In Nausikaa the only view we are given is Bloom's: his contact with Gerty is a kind of epiphany (305/372) – 'made me feel so young' (312/382). He is genuinely renewed: the citizen may not have meant to injure him (311/380); there is, even, no harm in Boylan (312/382). Like the novel itself, Bloom can always take another view.

In structure Nausikaa works up to Bloom's sight of Gerty's knickers, with accompanying fireworks, and from that moves down towards sleep with his interior monologue after orgasm, a portrait of the mind somnolent, wandering through half-formed thoughts, without connections and with abrupt transitions. Soporose Bloom demands a wide-awake reader who must supply content and context of thoughts that are left half-articulated. What is missing can often be supplied precisely, but Bloom's wandering logic and incomplete grammar also leave the reader plenty of interpretative space, as when Bloom considers a message in the sand: 'I. ... AM. A.' – 'a Jew'? 'a naughty boy'? (Bloom has just recalled the phrase from Martha's letter). But the reader need not stop with what Bloom might intend: Joyce's intention with the open space may be much wider. Bloom ended the previous episode as Elijah: forgiving his enemies (including the citizen who wanted to crucify him), with his thoughts on adultery and writing incomprehensibly on the ground (Gospel of John, 8), Bloom now resembles the Alpha and Omega whom Elijah typologically foreshadows.

14. *Oxen of the Sun (Odyssey, XII, 260–453)*

In Homer, when Odysseus's men kill the sacred cattle of Helios they commit a crime against fertility. This is one issue of Oxen of the Sun. The rowdy behaviour of Stephen and his cronies is utterly careless of Mrs Purefoy's pains in labour; the general ethos of their conversation shows a lack of reverence for physical life; their debasing of sex by divorcing it from love is epitomised by Mulligan's proposal to act as the stallion of a human stud-farm. In a letter to Frank Budgen, Joyce proposed, amongst other things, a simpler 'crime':

> Am working hard at *Oxen of the Sun*, the idea being the crime committed against fecundity by sterilizing the act of coition ... [*An account of the episode's various styles follows*] ... This procession is also linked back at each part subtly with some foregoing episode of the day and, besides this, with the natural stages of development in the embryo and the periods of faunal evolution in general ... Bloom is the spermatozoon, the hospital the womb, the nurse the ovum, Stephen the embryo. How's that for High? (*Letters*, I. 138–9)

Oxen of the Sun's comedy of style may be a better key to the episode's meaning than Joyce to Budgen, soberly interpreted. When Joyce wrote to Budgen the episode was in process. Much of the detail he mentions is changed in the novel. The letter's allegorisation seems tossed off in a spirit of technical bravura: it is not worked significantly into the novel. The links back to previous episodes (though present), and the stages of embryo development and faunal evolution (though traceable), are of minor importance.[12] 'How's that for High?' seems in the circumstances reasonable self-puncturing. The episode itself mentions contraception only in tones of very broad comedy: with a wonderful inappositeness, in the manner of *Pilgrim's Progress* (323/395); with the humorous innuendo of Sterne ((330/404) a French cloak is a condom, an umbrella a diaphragm); and in the pseudo-Carlyle slogan, 'Copulation without population! No, say I!'. Though Stuart Gilbert supposed Stephen's remarks on 'Godpossibled souls that we

nightly impossibilise' a denunciation of birth-control, they are
neither a denunciation nor about contraception. Stephen cannot
claim that they go to prostitutes 'nightly'. He would find
Boasthard the most modest of his titles. They are 'all prick and
no pence' (352/431), and could not afford it. But masturbation
is free. And Stephen does not denounce: he asks the company
for their theological view. Fecundity is hardly treated more
seriously. Mulligan is 'Le Fécondateur'. Theodore Purefoy is
the example of a fecundating patriarch: he is enjoined in
pseudo-Carlyle hectic rant to 'toil on'; he should feed his wife
meat to promote her sexual drive. Joyce is not wholly serious.
Bloom's earlier sceptical reflections on the Purefoys' annual
birth (132/161) are amply justified by the pains of Mrs Purefoy's
labour. The reader must decide whether the effect of all this is
to arraign sterilising coition as a crime against fecundity. Stanley
Sultan represents with the greatest solemnity the crime-of-
contraception view.[13] He is all at odds with the novel's tone.
When Joyce returned to the subject in *Finnegans Wake* it was
to enjoy the comedy of HCE's use of a condom (585), but the
commentator who finds there condemnation of a crime against
fecundity will have to grope his life long for this deep-hid
meaning in the true meinherr from Almany manner (*U*, 168/205).

In an episode so much concerned with birth and development,
it is important that Bloom and Stephen are seen as children,
and both in ways that mark continuity with as well as disjunction
from the present (337–8/412–14; 344/422). Also that Bloom
responds to Stephen in connection with his dead son (320/390).
This is Bloom and Stephen's first actual meeting, and Bloom's
movement towards adopting a son of his soul begins here.
'Orgulous of mother Church', Stephen is at his most irreligious.
He declares the Pope Vicar of Bray (accommodating all politics
out of self-interest), mocks the Virgin Birth, and parodies Christ
– foreshadowing his crucifixion, rejecting Satan in the desert,
and instituting the Eucharist (318–22/388–93). He blas-
phemously takes on the manner of God addressing Israel to
accuse Ireland of betraying him, and arraigns God in his
hangman and corpsechewer vein (342/420). Within the episode,

however, Stephen is condemned only from a perspective which is discredited by its naïve faith in scientific rationalism and its bland acceptance of individual suffering, a perspective which is, moreover, itself pointedly anti-religious (341–3/418–20, style of T. H. Huxley). In effect, Stephen's witty profanities are allowed to stand.

Oxen of the Sun is a history by parody of the development of English prose style.[14] Joyce's justification of the parodies – that the development of style parallels that of the foetus – is not crucial. Nor is the point of the parodies the learned pleasure of recognising styles. Not all are highly specific. What Joyce does need is for the reader to identify a style's usual parameters of subject-matter, and, as often elsewhere in the novel, to recognise the kind of sensibility or world view implied by a mode of language. Sometimes the comedy lies in working with the given style and applying it inventively to the material of *Ulysses* (Pepys's enthusiasm for miscellaneous detail and innocence of incongruity put to use with A. E., theosophist–farmer (325/398)). At other times the comedy comes from working against the style's usual content (the label on a bottle of Bass all but concealed as a mystical sign within a De Quincean opium fantasy (338/414)). Joyce also lets elements from outside a dominant style peep humorously through, as when, worked into late eighteenth-century magisterial moral reflection, we find linguistic motifs of Bloom (metempsychosis; his way of varying adages – 'birds of a feather laugh together'). And the style itself can produce behaviour to match: Dixon rebukes Punch Costello with grandly eighteenth-century manners. Oxen is the kind of thing in Joyce that bored D. H. Lawrence as 'too terribly would-be and done on purpose, utterly without spontaneity'.[15] It irritated even early apologists, such as Harry Levin.[16] It may be true that Oxen – like some of the more technical Homeric correspondences – does not grow much in the imagination. But Levin's irritation arose, I think, from wishing to take seriously Joyce's own ingenious justifications of the style in terms of embryonic development, and from expecting everything in the novel ultimately to refer to character and theme. Recent attention to the self-referentiality of language has tended to rehabilitate Joyce's exuberant experiments with style. But the pleasures of Oxen need not be intellectually stratospheric: Joyce aims to make the reader laugh.

15.   Circe (Odyssey, X)

Circe is an episode of purgation, for Bloom of sexual and for Stephen of religious guilt. As well as Rome, Stephen confronts England, while Bloom, in his rescue of Stephen, takes a first step to overcoming the major trauma of his life, the death of his son. The basic technique is dramatic: fantasies explore psychology, but also challenge accepted notions of character; they explore and comment on themes, but also break down norms of fiction with a delight in sheer formal and linguistic creativity.

Each of Bloom's fantasies is in some aspect psychological. They express his sexual tastes and guilts, and so are bound up with his impotence. They express his desire to be accepted and his fear of rejection, and so are bound up with his Jewishness. Feelings that exist, as it were, below the level of half-formed thoughts are extravagantly dramatised. Interior monologue is recast with normally submerged flickers of impulse or association and their histories built up into dialogue, with appropriate (often surreal) action and costume, and with a prodigal decoration of comic excrescence. It is a post-Freudian, Rabelaisian carnival. Bloom's first fantasy exhibits the method.[17] Bloom's unease in the brothel district is projected in terms of being caught by figures with whom he acts out scenes of guilt, inadequacy and embarrassment. With his parents Bloom reverts to childhood bases of adult furtiveness and guilt. With Molly his feelings of sexual inadequacy prompt grotesque exaggerations of grovelling submission – the attitude he later adopts in imagining his relation to Molly and Boylan as lovers. Respectable Mrs Breen denotes embarrassment, but as 'Josie Powell that was' she conjures up a compensating fantasy of debonaire virility: Bloom is squire of dames and (the Boylan role) Don Giovanni. Everyone role-plays with expressive costume and props. Bloom *père* is stage Jew in grammar and diction (Germanic and Yiddish), Isaac fumbling the sonface of Bloom–Jacob. Bloom *mère* is stage Irishwoman, with Agnus Dei, shrivelled potato and appropriate idiom. Molly in Turkish costume epitomises Bloom's oriental yearnings, Ithacan and sensuous (Agendath Netaim, opulent curves). Her trousers express her relationship with Bloom ('Wore the breeches. Suppose she does' (312/381)), and his sexual taste for dominant women, which later fantasies develop. The appeal of Ulysses for Joyce was the comprehensiveness of his personality, and this Ulysses goes further than his model. He is hoggishly transformed by Bella–Circe. He desires upper-class women whose social power, horsey recreations and self-righteous prosecution-cum-persecution are full of barely suppressed sexual violence (Joyce invokes Sacher–Masoch whose *Venus in Furs* – on dominance, violence and desire – is one source of Circe). Masochism and sadism are two sides of the same coin, as in Bloom's repeated (false) supposition that a nun invented barbed wire. Bloom is also a voyeur. He has tried cross-dressing, which Joyce expands into a full desire to change sex. Bloom's fantasies admit masturbation only in a way which expresses continued guilt and furtiveness by nicely obscure or euphemistic expression (405, 1872–8/496; 448, 3353/549). A desire perhaps connected with buttocks proves stinkingly repugnant beyond obscurity or euphemism.[18]

Bloom's fantasies of sexual guilt are compensated by others of fulfilment based on his social schemes. From reviled outcast he becomes celebrated hero. Wish-fulfilment also collapses into the fears that feed it: Bloom as new Messiah becomes, as in Cyclops, the reviled and martyred Scapegoat. But as Messiah, and via Shakespeare, Bloom is comically identified with Stephen (488/598; 463/567). He enters Stephen's recollected dream to Stephen's cry of '*Pater*! Free!'. The brothel–Purgatory prepares Bloom to assert himself. He is the dark horse who wins the Ascot Gold Cup (467/573; 275/335). As the final visionary connection of Stephen and Rudy indicates – not without comedy – Bloom is ready to adopt a son of his soul.

Stephen's purgation is briefer. He must 'kill the priest and the king': confront the church (in the person of his dead mother) and the state (alias Private Carr). Stephen's hallucination of his mother forces him into postures of heroic defiance unlike *A Portrait*'s recipes of evasion, repeated by Shem/Glugg in *Finnegans Wake* – silence, exile and cunning (*P*, 251; *FW*, 228). Stephen is Siegfried bringing about the Dusk of the Gods (457/560; 475/583). He is Lucifer refusing to serve the corpsechewer God who inflicted his mother's suffering. For Stephen's mother, religion is the threat of punishment. Stephen's view is quite different. It is one of the controversial recuperations of the Gabler edition that Stephen knows, in theory, the answer to the eager demand he makes of his mother: the word known to all men is Love (161). What Stephen needs from his mother is not the word but the meaning – how to turn his Aquinan tags into emotional substance. It is a subject on which Rescuer Bloom, potential surrogate parent, has already made his profession (273/332–3). Stephen's confrontation with the English state is contrastingly anti-heroic: Stephen would evade it if he could. Epitomes of England and Ireland indicate the symbolic nature of this brawl outside a brothel. Edward VII celebrates the hanging of the Croppy Boy (like Stephen the Croppy did not pray for his mother). The citizen calls on the Holy Spirit to avenge nationalist executions; Old Gummy Granny offers religious sanction for nationalist violence. But she is, to Stephen, a betrayer, 'the old sow that eats her farrow'. Against force his (unsuccessful) weapon is 'pure reason'. Again, this recalls Bloom in Cyclops. Stephen meets, too, with a similar fate. The narrative identifies 'heroic' nationalist and British soldier as Bloom and Stephen are drawn together through contrary attitudes and ethics.

Bloom's fantasies and Stephen's hallucination have psychological aspects. Not everything in Circe, however, can be understood in psychological terms. Tone and form are as important as dramatised psychology. When Bloom's unpaid-for soap becomes a sun and jingles a rhyme in Bloom's praise, when Molly's supposed taste for the exotic, as exemplified by negro servants, Othello, sweeps, and so on, becomes a black-and-white minstrel act, these are turns of the screw of absurdity whose meaning is their comic tone. The processes of fantasising give ample scope for Joyce's sense of the ludicrous in the witty creation of bathetic disjunctions: Bloom as philanthropist, Bloom as lapsed Jew, Bloom who 'ate with relish ... inner organs', unite in the pork kidney form of the New Bloomusalem. Plausible fantasy (lord mayor) is subjected to the comic scrutiny of absurd inflation – 'emperor president and king chairman': every authority role seized, the last the most petty. Bloom's social projects of the grandest inclusiveness (union of Jew, Moslem and gentile) comically settle purely personal scores (no more patriotism of bar spongers). His uniting of Israel and Ireland is grotesquely symbolised in the Kol Nidre played by a pipe and drum band. Hero of parliamentary and revolutionary parties, he unites the irreconcilable (he is the new Parnell and the man who got away James Stephens), but Nova Hibernia also finds Catholic and Protestant bating nothing of their rival claims (391,1420–23/480).

The transformation of man to beast by a magic conventionally allegorised as sensual indulgence is one subject of Homer's Circe. Joyce's Circe extends this: humans become beasts (Bloom as hog and dark horse; Stephen as hunted fox; Simon Dedalus as buzzard/heraldic eagle; Bella with goatish cloven hoof); beasts become human (the dog/Dignam; the antlered hat-rack/ Shakespeare); beasts become other beasts (the spaniel-retriever-setter-wolfdog-mastiff which pursues Bloom in ever-shifting manifestations). Most of all, in keeping with the surreal and dream-like quality of the action as well as the drunkenness of the characters, things take on personalities. Remarks from the gas-jets seem pure surrealism. Bella's speaking fan expresses Bloom's perception of its owner. When the brothel wallpaper enters Bloom's fantasy of the *Photo–Bits* Nymph, the effect is dream-like: an outside stimulus is woven into material generated by the psyche. When the same wallpaper files across country in the Stephen fox-hunt, the effect is of surrealist cinematic collage. And when the brothel oilcloth is choreographed by Professor

Maginni into a dance of the hours, the effect is of drunkenness.
But animations of the inanimate cannot be neatly placed. In
Circe nothing stays in place in either real or fantasy worlds:
garlic on a prostitute's breath transforms the New Jerusalem
into a city of tombs (389/477); urine in a chamber pot adapts
to its Nymph-and-yews context to become a waterfall (446/547).
Words fall apart to re-combine, as in a Freudian dream, or in
Finnegans Wake: 'Namine. Jacobs. Vobiscuits'.[19] It is all part
of the controlled anarchy that expresses disorientation for
Bloom, Stephen and the reader.

The fantasies of Circe are part psychological, part tonal and
formal. They can also be seen as a mode of thematic commentary,
though the recapitulations of Circe are always from new
perspectives which, in their challenge to values apparently
established earlier, indicate the difficulty of situating Joyce
amongst the rival voices. The heroism of Tom Rochford, a
positive aspect of Dublin in Wandering Rocks, is here treated
with mock-heroic Cuchulain-myth comedy (387/474; 488/598).
Bloom's feeding of the gulls, an indication of his compassionate
nature in Lestrygonians, is pointedly juxtaposed with Bob
Doran's drunkenly sentimental attitude to animals (370/454;
251/305). Most of all, Bloom's social attitudes, the moral centre
of Joyce's anti-nationalist critique in Cyclops, become material
for comedy. They are subject to further revision in Eumaeus
(525–6/643). Locating some Joycean centre is evidently at least
complex. Still, the fantasies of Circe do seem at times oblique
commentary. When Tennyson joins Privates Carr and Compson,
'*In Union Jack blazer and cricket flannels* ... Theirs not to
reason why', Joyce surely comments on Tennyson and soldiers:
Tennyson's poetry is armchair jingoism which shields itself from
intelligent critique by an appeal to patriotism; its sentimental
praise of courage blurs an accurate perception of military
stupidity and the suffering involved in violence. These are
Joycean extrapolations, but one had better beware of reading
in one's own predispositions. When anti-Bloomite Hugh Kenner
seizes upon '*lugubru Booloohoom*' as 'defining the carressing
self-pity of lugubrious Bloom'[20] he fails to register that the phrase

expresses an evident distortion, and that '*lugubru Booloohoom*' in a concave mirror is complemented by '*jollypoldly*' in a convex (354/434). Joyce's point is not what Kenner paraphrases but what he exhibits, what Bloom's thematic puzzling about parallax draws attention to: perception and point of view are not separable.

Because of Circe's quasi-dramatic form, the challenges of *Ulysses* to ideas of character in more conventional fiction are here at their most obvious – challenges to the notion of unique individual identities suggested by the 'metempsychosis' motif, the Homeric parallels, the echoes between Bloom and Stephen; challenges to the stability and coherence of identity implied by the nature of interior monologue and resulting from the formal position of Circe: as climax of the Odyssey it is transindividual summary. Bloom's fantasies draw on the novel beyond his consciousness; other fantasies draw on Bloom. Reappearances are recapitulations, not by a character, but for the reader. The technique is clear at the climax of drunken dancing (472/579): fragments from Wandering Rocks, Aeolus, Proteus, Nausikaa, Lotus-Eaters and Cyclops cannot be located in any single consciousness. It is a drunken glimpse of the novel so far, given – with its piglings, hogs, and Gadarene swine – in Circean transformation. Role-playing too destabilises individual identity. To himself in interior dialogue Stephen is Philip Drunk and Philip Sober. To the soldiers he is 'the parson', to the prostitutes (prompted by Bloom), 'the professor'. Bloom especially appears in many guises. '*Virag truculent ... Grave Bloom ... Henry gallant*' juxtaposes three forms of Bloom, each a composite. Virag, ancestor and brothel moth, is a dramatisation of Bloom's Herr Professor Luitpold Blumenduft personality (250/304), a pretence that his interest in sex is respectably scientific. Henry resembles the tenor Mario (Bloom thinks of him in Aeolus), who resembles the Saviour; his dulcimer is a Bloomish property (47/57), but his quasi-Spanish costume is Bloomian anti-type: confident exotic lover. Many of Circe's fractured components of Poldy are past Blooms, forms of self about which Stephen has repeatedly raised the problem of continuity: 'I am other I now ... But I, entelechy, form of forms, am I by memory because under unchanging forms'.[21] *Ulysses* does not simply endorse this Aristotelian solution. Circe juxtaposes past and present to show continuity by memory, but suggests too that pasts we apparently remember are in fact reconstructed on the basis of the present, a view of memory also described by Stephen (160, 383–5/194). When Bloom recalls wooing Josie Powell with 'Love's old sweet song' and '*Là ci darem*' it is not because he did so once but because he conceives of Molly and Boylan as doing so now. When present transforms past in this way the continuities apparently established by memory become less secure than they at first seem. The present, with its fantasy alternative selves, offers no secure cohesive identity either. How possible the unrealised ever was is likewise a problem that has absorbed Stephen (21/25), but realisation is not wholly the issue: whether conceived as possible (Stephen, Cardinal Dedalus – because in *A Portrait* Stephen considers becoming a priest), or yearned for though impossible ('what you longed for has come to pass': Bloom in female form), roads fate did not take still haunt the individual's self-conception. Selves disintegrate in the Circean crucible: Stephen and Bloom, who echo one another throughout the novel, are most closely identified immediately before Stephen's crisis and Bloom's rescue: Stephen repeats Bloom in his own person and in his hallucination of his mother.[22] Metempsychosis, Odysseus–Bloom, Stoom/Blephen: 'one life is' (again) 'all' (230/280). It is a sense of the individual taken much further in the intermingling dream identities of *Finnegans Wake*.

III   NOSTOS

16.   *Eumaeus (Odyssey, XIV–XVI)*

As in Homer, where Ulysses presents himself in disguise to his old herdsman, the subject of Eumaeus is imposture: imposture

of people, things, and language. Able seaman Murphy is the
main impostor: were his recounted exploits true he would be a
Ulysses – but, very likely, they are not. In this literal sense, as
a great traveller, Bloom too is an impostor-Ulysses: his travels
are plans only, and grotesquely unUlyssean in nature. The theme
re-echoes everywhere. The keeper of the cabman's shelter may
or may not be Skin-the-Goat Fitzharris the Invincible, accomplic
e to the Phoenix Park murders. 'Lord' John Corley's relation
to the Talbots de Malahide is doubtful. So is the relation of
Simon Dedalus the circus sharpshooter to Stephen's father. The
cabby who uncannily resembles townclerk, Henry Campbell, is
a variation on this theme, as are 'the socalled roll' and 'an
untasteable apology for a cup of coffee' (both with numerous
ingenious variants). Language too is 'imposture' (509/622):
obscenely blasphemous haggling about money sounds to Bloom
so musical that it inspires a rhapsody about poetry and the good
life, a rhapsody which is itself marked by imposture with its
pseudo-Italian and 'freely' translated misquotation. English is
not so readily misunderstood, but Bloom's splendidly humorous
misinterpretations of Stephen's 'simple' (518/634) or of
Herrick's *protestant* (540/661) indicate how important context
is to meaning, even in one's own language. Unfamiliar with the
appropriate frames of reference, though Bloom recognises the
words he no more understands their meanings than he understands
the apparently lyrical *puttana madonna* (whore of a Blessed
Virgin). But Bloom also points shifts of meaning by context:
though he recognises that Stephen is not 'orthodox' in social–
romantic terms he comically supposes that 'orthodox' can be
used of Stephen in another sense (536/656; 526/644).

The narrative voice in Eumaeus recalls the Gerty MacDowell
section of Nausikaa, but while the Nausikaa stereotypes of
language and feeling are derived from romantic fiction, the
Eumaeus narrator deals in clichés from the classics: Virgil,
Shakespeare and Milton all make allusive appearances, though
with an air not of direct reading but of parading a common
currency ('as the Latin poet remarks' after not-quite Virgil; 'as
someone somewhere says' after not-quite Milton). Like the long

drifting sentences in which Bloom's hazy thoughts are reported, like the narrator's habit of becoming stuck on a word,[23] cliché characterises tiredness. It also unites tiredness and imposture: ready-made phrases are the tired mind's falsification of experience. Joyce points to a similar tendency in narrative: the newspaper report of Dignam's funeral is a mixture of invention, inaccuracy, accident and advertisement; and, though the first is 'fact' and the second 'strict history', Bloom's two reports of rescuing Parnell's hat are different. History does indeed repeat itself (535/655), in more than one sense (particular: Bloom rescues headgear (95/115); general: Bloom is Ulysses). But also, history repeated is changed. '*Telegraph*, tell a graphic lie' is linguistic play not just applicable to sensational journalism.

The narrator of Eumaeus is not only a mode of language. He is a character, humorous in his variations on 'sailor' (Sinbad, Shipahoy, the old tarpaulin, the ancient mariner), fussy in his attempt to give accurately the Malahide background of Corley. He is not, as the first Nausikaa narrator is, entirely identified with one character's mode of seeing. He is not Bloom. His clichés half-fit Bloom's (whose speech can be reported through them as Stephen's cannot). Bloom goes beyond and criticises them (the narrator piles cliché on cliché; in the indirectly reported speech of Bloom the set phrase is, as elsewhere, humorously varied ('Love me, love my dirty shirt')). Bloom likewise punctures the offered conventions of feeling and situation: the journalese view of Parnell and Kitty O'Shea (535/655), whom he nevertheless sees partly in terms of a stereotype to which he is more subject (Latin countries are hot-blooded (Spain: Kitty/Molly)). As in Nausikaa, cliché is not easily escaped. Bloom is implicated: Bloom's scepticism and humour somewhat free him. Similarly with imposture. In referring to the Cyclops fracas Bloom presents himself, with a considerable degree of arrangement, in terms suited to impress Stephen (525/634), but he is also an accurate sceptic seeing through the stories of Impostor Murphy.

Eumaeus is the first episode in which the direct relationship of Stephen and Bloom, the 'fusion' of which Joyce speaks in the Linati schema, begins to be established. For most of the episode they are comically at odds, over religion, politics, and art, but the reader can enjoy the comedy of these initial failures of communication while recognising that none of them points to the central or whole truth in any area. Though Stephen, falling in with the theme of imposture, plays the role of official church spokesman, his views on the Church and on the '*dio boia*', the 'corpsechewer' who 'wants blood victim', are not dissimilar to Bloom's. Though there are more profound differences between their political views these are not so great as the clash between Bloom's comfortably hopeful liberal egalitarianism and Stephen's uncompromising individualism suggest: they are at one in their view of the basic justice of the nationalist case, and in their attitude to political violence (525/643). In their comically ill-assorted musical opinions both are swanking: Bloom's absurd judgements on 'light opera of the *Don Giovanni* description' and 'the severe classical school such as Mendelssohn' are as much Eumaeus-imposture as Stephen's plan to buy a Dolmetsch lute. But both love music: their different tastes are a function of their different educations. Clearly Joyce means there are great barriers between them, as there always are between people except in romantic fiction. But despite differences of age, temperament, education and outlook Stephen and Bloom have their moment of communion (514/629). Bloom always considers material aspects of the most emotional subjects (will Boylan pay Molly? (303/369)), and he accordingly considers the material possibilities of his relationship with Stephen, but to say that this is all that is involved[24] denies the plain sense of much of the episode. Bloom's care of Stephen is, at the least, fatherly. His half-formed plans for Stephen and Molly may intimate possibilities of deeper friendship. Though Stephen cannot see this for himself, Joyce indicates in Stephen's song, '*Youth here has End*' (the song is used in the same way in the final section of *Giacomo Joyce*), that his new relationship, at least potentially, marks an important point of transition. What Bloom half-consciously recognises in the parallel vision of Rudy (497/609) Stephen unconsciously registers in his choice of music.

17. Ithaca (Odyssey, XVII–XXII)

> I am writing *Ithaca* in the form of a mathematical catechism.
> All events are resolved into their cosmic physical, psychical etc.
> equivalents ... so that not only will the reader know everything
> and know it in the baldest coldest way, but Bloom and Stephen
> thereby become heavenly bodies, wanderers like the stars at
> which they gaze. (*Letters*, I, 159–60)

Knowing everything in the baldest, coldest way may not seem
immediately attractive, but Ithaca was Joyce's favourite section
of *Ulysses*.[25] Its delights are partly stylistic. Though the reader
can lapse into the position of Bloom when he understands
Stephen 'Not verbally. Substantially' (572/697), to grasp only
the gist is to miss the point. One pleasure of Ithaca lies in
following precisely Joyce's playfully structured paragraphs and
struggling with his, at times, deliberately opaque language. In
its rhythms, verbal music and other aspects of rhetorical
structure the style is often like the quasi-free verse of Renaissance
prose retuned for comic effects. The language can be play of
sound almost independent of meaning. It can also conceal
meaning, in diction (unusual words, coinages, and technical or
specialised vocabulary), and in grammar:

> the natural grammatical transition by inversion involving no
> alteration of sense of an aorist preterite proposition (parsed as
> masculine subject, monosyllabic onomatopoeic transitive verb
> with direct feminine object) from the active voice into its
> correlative aorist preterite proposition (parsed as feminine
> subject, auxiliary verb and quasimonosyllabic onomatopoeic past
> participle with complementary masculine agent) in the passive
> voice ... (604/734)

That is: he fucked her; she was fucked by him. The studiedly
scientific manner of Ithaca variously parodies the claims of
science to give total explanations and the epic intention of
including all knowledge. And, though Joyce was himself so very
careful with realism of fictional surface, even within this very
section (*Letters*, I, 175; 546, 84–9/668), while his care with

surfaces indicates the partial validity of realism, the attention to language as self-referential play and as opaque screen combines with the immense paraphernalia of detail to undercut realism's claim simply to mirror a non-fictional world: the more detail Joyce includes the more we recognise the inexhaustibility of what might be given and the narrowness of the selection that usually is. Attention to language as a self-enclosed system and attention to the human content that, on another view, language embodies are often held to be mutually exclusive. Joyce exuberantly exploits the potential in language for systematised play, and he was evidently aware of the problems of language as mediator between world and consciousness. But, unlike some of his expositors, Joyce saw language as self-referential only within limits, and was comic about this, not pompous. Beneath all its parade of problems of the medium, Ithaca is the climax of central aspects of the novel's human content.

The attitude to Bloom in Ithaca is an epitome of the novel's mixture of sympathy and irony: 'jocoserious' is Joyce's word (553/677). Various main strands of his character are repeated in humorous ways. He is the new womanly man again in his views on children's toys (no militaristic ones (559/683)). His bourgeois ambitions are presented satirically, though they have too their humane side: conditions for servants in Flowerville are unusually generous for 1904. His habitual final meditation before sleep – the ultimate advertisement (592/720) – is pure comedy. But comedy is not the dominant tone. The aspirations for a more just society which lie behind the emperor president and king chairman fantasies of Circe make a sober reappearance (571–2/696–7). And Bloom's religious speculations, based on his view of the physical nature of the universe (573–5/698–700), are not impugned by his errors of fact. Though Bloom is in some ways wrong in terms of knowledge in 1904 (Joyce simply does not make him improbably well-informed) this does not invalidate the drift of his view. His figures on the vastness of space are all underestimates: more accurate knowledge would only strengthen his arguments. Bloom is a representative late Victorian sceptic in the views he draws from his 'facts': that there may be life elsewhere than on earth; that – supposing such life to be not different in kind morally from life as we know it – this possibility gives rise to religious problems (Christ can scarcely be supposed to undertake multiple Incarnations); 'That it was not a heaventree, not a heavengrot, not a heavenbeast, not a heavenman'. That these conclusions have been supposed by non-sceptical critics to condemn Bloom is rather the novel's verdict on them.[26] Though he is an outsider, Bloom is often representative of his age. Ithaca also emphasises the wider representative status that the Odyssean parallels constantly imply. That Bloom's day can be described in terms of aspects of the Jewish liturgical calendar (599/728–9) – as it was earlier in a parody of the Catholic litany (407/498–9) – is primarily comic: we are more aware of parodic inventiveness than true archetype of situation. But the tone is quite different when Bloom's singing of a Hebrew melody evokes 'The traditional figure of hypostasis ... The traditional accent of the ecstasy of catastrophe' (565/689). He is wandering Israel, the wandering planet into which it was the aim of the Ithacan manner to transform him, and, finally, 'Everyman' (598/727).

Beneath its 'baldest coldest' manner Ithaca contains some of the novel's most emotional moments for Bloom, as when parting from Stephen provokes thoughts of death (as it does too for Stephen (578,1230–31/704)). Or, more fully written, when Bloom is reminded of his father's suicide (594–6/723–5). That such moments are usually contextualised by, often interwoven with, comedy does not decrease their pathos. Bloom's memories of his father are immediately juxtaposed with his fantasised reduction to 'lunatic pauper'. Splendidly comic in its crescendo of states of indigence, and in its enjoyment of the vocabulary of beggary ('marfeast, lickplate'), it is a comic juxtaposition which is itself inwoven with non-comic materials: the humour of manner is qualified by reminders of real gradations of poverty shown in the novel – debt collector, sandwichman, blind stripling, maimed sailor. The positive view of Bloom is at its strongest in the Odyssean centre of Ithaca, the slaying of the suitors. Frank Budgen reports Joyce's difficulty with the basic conception of Ithaca because the slaughter of the suitors in Homer seemed to Joyce an unUlyssean action for which his own hatred of bloodshed made it difficult to find an equivalent.[27] Joyce's eventual solution is a brilliant adaptation of the *Odyssey* to his own ethics, echoing in Bloom at the personal level the opposition to brute force in politics for which he is attacked in Cyclops. Bloom is an ideally Joycean Odysseus, slaying metaphorically, by non-violence, making Boylan irrelevant by his preponderant reactions of abnegation and equanimity. Bloom's acceptance of adultery may not please Joyce's Catholic critics, but it is clear from *Exiles* that, with regard to individual sexual freedom, Joyce had only more revolutionary views than Bloom.

Bloom and Stephen represent opposite temperaments – 'The scientific. The artistic' (558/683). As a father in search of a son and a son in search of a father they also have much in common. Ithaca shows finally how much. The parallels which, taking up the theme of John F. Taylor and Stephen's Parable of the Plums, they elaborate between England and Ireland (563–5/687–9) prepare the ground. Both belong to oppressed races from which both are alienated and of which both have an imperfect knowledge of the history and language. Stephen's ballad of the Christian boy murdered by a Jewess confirms the analogy: Stephen is the boy gone to a Jew's house; phrases used of the boy are repeated of Bloom; Bloom is the sometime victim of sectarian violence. Their performance of the psalm *In exitu Israel* implies what they have to gain from each other. The psalm – which in itself connects Bloom and Stephen: Bloom has twice misremembered it (101/122; 310/378) – commemorates the exodus from Egypt, an event which typologically foreshadows Christ's release of mankind from bondage to sin. In Hebrew and Christian terms it is the archetypal act of liberation. Stephen's performance is, of course, mocking. Whether the reader should see in Stephen's mockery a significance beyond his grasp, Joyce leaves the whole novel to decide. Certainly the fruit of Bloom and Stephen's exit is a very Joycean affirmation of communion: they urinate together. It seems unnecessary to

insist on Joyce's quirky association of excretion and creativity
– though Bloom puns on 'chamber music' as Joyce did in the
title of his first publication (232/282). The great pee is one of
the moments of Ithaca marked by its emotional treatment in
the context of the predominantly unemotional style. It follows
Bloom's attempt to 'elucidate the mystery' of Molly to Stephen,
'with subdued affection and admiration', an attempt which
leaves each 'contemplating the other in both mirrors of the
reciprocal flesh of theirhisnothis fellowfaces'. Joyce strains the
language to show how closely together Bloom and Stephen are
drawn. The incident is Joyce's equivalent of Lawrence's
'Gladiatorial', the male communion through naked wrestling
of *Women in Love*. But where Lawrence is extraordinary,
extravagantly flouting taboos, Joyce is ordinary but none the
less transgressive, violating the convention that this ordinary
situation is non-sexual. Both Bloom and Stephen are conscious
of the other's sexual organ, though as their communion lapses
Joyce brings out with his usual humour the differences in spite
of which it was achieved (577, 1199–1209/702–3).

18. Penelope (Odyssey, XXIII)

> *Penelope* is the clou ('star turn') of the book ... It turns like the
> huge earth ball slowly surely and evenly round and round
> spinning, its four cardinal points being the female breasts, arse,
> womb and cunt expressed by the words *because, bottom* (in all
> senses bottom button, bottom of the class, bottom of the sea,
> bottom of his heart), *woman, yes*. Though probably more
> obscene than any preceding episode it seems to me to be perfectly
> sane full amoral fertilisable untrustworthy engaging shrewd
> limited prudent indifferent *Weib* ('woman'). (*SL*, 285)

Just as Bloom is 'Everyman', Joyce means to point beyond
Molly individually and so associates her with a spectrum of
female mythic types. Born on the Feast of the Nativity of the
Blessed Virgin, Molly enters *Ulysses* as Calypso. In Ithaca she
is connected with the Greek and Roman earth goddesses, Gea
and Tellus. Now she is Penelope. As with many of the Homeric
parallels, the obvious effect of Molly as Penelope, not only

accepting her suitor but relishing sex with him in the most physical way, is ironic. As with other identifications, there is, too, a deeper significance which is unironic. Though physically unfaithful to Bloom, and unsentimentally critical of what she regards as his oddities, Molly is faithful to him emotionally, as the final drift of her monologue indicates.

The acclaim given to the portrait of Molly has had sometimes an embarrassingly triumphant air of finding certain stereotypical views of women justified by it (see, for example, Carl Jung in *Letters*, III, 253). But Joyce chose as his hero a figure who openly combats and obliquely undermines stereotypes of masculinity, ✓ and he complements this in his central female character. Molly inhabits some conventional views of women, but she shrewdly punctures others. She has no women friends and sees other women as rivals, either sexual (Mary Driscoll, Josie Powell), or professional (Kathleen Kearney). Her relationship with Hester Stanhope however, which is a central memory of her life, though it includes emotional rivalry, also indicates a quite different possibility: intense affection. Molly is subject to women's magazine views of fashion and beauty, which she also criticises (618/750; 622/755). She sees love as the central business of a woman's life and is capable of sentimental idealising, as in the images she fantasises around Stephen. But conventional or idealising views are complemented by her shrewd sense and frankly physical attitude to sex. And, though Molly would disdain the title, she is in some ways a proto-feminist. Her attitude to her profession is utterly off-hand (she has not performed in public for a year, and regards breathing exercises in the light of their advantage to the figure), but that she has a profession is unusual for her time and gives her some independence. She is scornful of reactionary anti-feminist views on 'womens higher functions'. And her low view of most men can take an ur-feminist turn on the consequences for civilisation of male dominance (640,1434–9/778).

'How many lovers had Molly Bloom?' may seem a question of the 'How many children had Lady Macbeth?' type, and one could well leave it alone if some critics had not striven to prove, against the obvious reading of Molly's uninhibited sexual explicitness, that the answer is none.[28] The argument depends on Bloom's list of her lovers – or admirers – which it is supposed includes nobody before Boylan with whom she has actually had intercourse (601–2/731). A precise combing of the text shows that Molly undertook a range of activities with the men listed, beginning colourfully with the manipulation to orgasm of lieutenant Mulvey when she was fifteen. The list is mixed, and includes men utterly rejected, but there is no telling what Molly did with all those on it. (It seems unlikely, for example, that she would make so dramatic a fuss about merely kissing Bartell d'Arcy (614/745)). More important, the list is apparently Bloom's and partially ignorant. It should not be taken solemnly: it is, in part, a joke against Bloom, who is complacently supposing his own knowledge not subject to the limitations he observes in others. Molly mentions various other men, the most important of whom is lieutenant Stanley Gardner. Bloom apparently knows nothing about Gardner, though Molly's relationship with him was evidently sexual[29] and ended only when he went to the Boer War – that is, when Molly and Bloom had been married for over a decade. The evident sense of Molly's monologue, a sense for which the Dublin gossip about her has prepared – that her sex-life has been racy and independent – is not to be gainsaid by combing the text to prove that she has not had, in the scientific phraseology of Ithaca, 'complete carnal knowledge' of the men on Bloom's list. The attempt to confine Molly's lovers within the term 'admirers' smells of an unJoycean puritanism, though it may point obliquely to a truth – that Joyce wished Molly to appeal to a wide range of views and so left possible the interpretation that has hardened into dogma.

Because the texture of mental life that Joyce depicts would be belied by the usual formalisations of writing, every aspect of Molly's language emphasises its spoken quality: her dialectisms, vernacular sayings, and misuse of words (usually by phonetic analogy), her tendency to call on ready-made phrases from her song repertoire, and above all her unpunctuated grammatical incompletion. Though the formalisations of writing are inappropriate, if the reader is to perceive Molly's thought as it must be supposed to occur to her her words have to be organised into their syntactic relationships. The problems of doing this arise from the sudden breaks, turns and odd conjunctions which characterise Molly's thought. It is a problem rich in comic possibilities. When, in thinking of a statue of the Virgin and Child, Molly switches to Edward VII's mistress, Lillie Langtrey, and her chastity belt (619/752), the obvious humour lies in the disjunction, BVM/LL. This is heightened by the process of reading. First because the Virgin and the mistress overlap: only in failing to find a sense for 'how could she go to the chamber' do we grasp that Our Lady has ceased to be Molly's subject. And then the need continuously to work out syntax enforces slower reading and so gives full effect to the comedy of Joyce's details: Molly passes from the Virgin to Lillie Langtrey via the connection, physical problems in the genital area: giving birth (the statue Jesus is too big), urinating (how do you get the belt off?). Molly's fragmentary grammar is full of meanings. The comedy of their discovery-cum-construction is high among Penelope's pleasures.

Though the main subject of Molly's monologue is Molly herself she also turns us back to Everyman–Bloom, to enforce the positive view of him and all he represents that the novel as a whole takes. The striking similarities in content, tone and structural position with the final monologue of ALP in *Finnegans Wake* bring this out clearly. Querulous, even profoundly disappointed with life – though also responsive as Gea–Tellus –Molly is to the beauty of nature (a rare but important tone in Joyce, as with Stephen on the beach in *A Portrait*, IV) – ALP bears away a leaf to remind her of earth as she, the river, merges back into her old father, the sea. As with Molly, 'yes' is a key word in her ending. Conscious of all life's faults and failures, both accept it positively. It is the right Joycean note.

2

'Extravagant Excursions into Forbidden Territory': Bloom, Stephen and the Joycean Triangle

Joyce knew from the example of writers he most admired – Flaubert, Ibsen, Wilde – that writing can excite moral resistance because it embodies moral discovery. So it is with sex and the banning of *Ulysses*. Joyce deplored the falsity on which moral hysteria about sex is based. His own directness is at least a rediscovery in morals, and one needed in 1920 from Joyce's point of view without the puritanical mystico-religious overlay which sanctions sex in D. H. Lawrence: that prevents clear thought about sex as surely as any Victorian holy horror. It would be a displacement of the same error to be portentously high-minded about the treatment of sex in *Ulysses*. It gives rise to some of Joyce's best comedy, which gains much of its zest from breaking taboos. But it is also an aspect of Joyce's project to promote freedom of consciousness. Like his admired Ibsen, Joyce let in fresh air. Though the sexual ethos Joyce opposes had a specifically Irish Catholic dimension, not only Ireland is to change by being able to see itself. Anthony Cronin comments well that it is the mark of a great writer to extend the field of recorded human experience. In extending what is recorded the writer also provides models of alternative modes of being.

As a challenge to myths of sexual normality Joyce includes, without fuss, a wide range of sexual feelings and behaviour: heterosexual sex with a strongly physical emphasis between

Molly and Boylan; heterosexual sex problems (Bloom's impotence); sex in adolescence (Molly's reminiscences; Gerty Mac-
Dowell titillating Bloom); masturbation (Bloom, Molly, and
others): prostitution (at Bella Cohen's); pornography (books
for Molly, photos for Bloom); cross-dressing, sadism, masochism and voyeurism (Bloom, in fantasy); homosexuality, and
bisexuality (Richard Best and Wilde; Shakespeare). (Best –
'tame essence of Wilde' – is compared with the young man of
Shakespeare's sonnets, and with Phaedo, the young companion
of Socrates (163/198; 177/215): Wilde had famous forebears.)
It is only when homogenic love dare not speak its name, so
Joyce implies, that it expresses itself with Wilde's mannered
flamboyance. Joyce tended to think of exclusive homosexuality
as socially induced: Wilde was a product of the English public
school system (*Letters*, II, 199; *CW*, 204). In *Ulysses* homosexual
feeling is part of the experience of people who are predominantly
heterosexual: Molly in her friendship with Hester Stanhope;
Cranly and Mulligan in their friendships with Stephen.[1] It is
part, too, of Bloom's relationship with Stephen.

This is not at all to suggest that Bloom is suppressedly
homosexual: that is Mulligan's view. Having earlier met Bloom
inspecting sculptured buttocks in the National Museum he
interprets Bloom's interest in Stephen with his usual coarse
simplicity: 'get thee a breech pad' (179/217). Joyce implies rather
an extension of Freud's view that both hetero and homosexuality
represent a narrowing from a pre-pubescent 'freedom to range
equally over male and female objects'.[2] On this view psychological development corresponds with the physiological: as
Joyce recorded in the Oxen notesheets, 'Embryo 1st asexual'.[3]
It is characteristic of the Joycean artist to be in some way
transsexual. Ibsen's great female characters are evidence of 'a
curious mixture of the woman in his nature' (*CW*, 64). Stephen
mocks androgyny (*U*, 213/175), but is himself androgynous (*SH*,
27; *U*, 458/561). In one of the epiphanies transferred to *A Portrait*
he is mistaken for a girl (*P*, 70). Shakespeare, in Scylla and
Charybdis, is bisexual, and, like God the Father, gives birth by
a sort of male parthenogenesis (his child is his work). This

reflects Joyce's way of imaging his own creation, and the work of the artist generally: the imagination is a womb (*Letters*, II, 308; *P*, 221). That there is 'a touch of the artist about old Bloom' (193/235) draws him into this portrait of the artist as transsexual, but transsexual characteristics are not confined to the artist. In *Finnegans Wake* HCE is of 'the old middlesex party' (523). His initials show his 'homosexual catheis of empathy' (522). Tried for a sexual crime – taking 'epscene licence ... as regards them male privates'[4] – he is parallel to Wilde.

In Bloom, Joyce draws together these explorations of sexual identity and sexual feeling outside the usual categories. To the loafers in Kiernan's bar Bloom is 'one of those mixed middlings' (old middlesex party), 'lying up ... once a month with headache like a totty with her courses' (277/338). To Dixon, Bloom is 'the new womanly man'. To Mulligan, he is 'bisexually abnormal'.[5] In Cyclops, Bloom opposes the stereotypically male ethos by which enjoyment of violent sports passes readily into admiration for violent self-assertion in social and political life. In Oxen of the Sun he is the exception to a general male indifference to the suffering of women in childbirth, a feeling comically extended in the Circe fantasies when Bloom changes sex, longs to be a mother, and gives birth. Bloom's 'masculine feminine passive active hand' (551/674) is, like his female middle name (594/723), what Joyce in *Dubliners* calls a gnomon: the part figures in miniature the whole.

Bloom's interest in Stephen is first of all as a surrogate for the son for whom Bloom still hopes, tentatively but intensely (234/285). Stephen might stand in place of the dead Rudy, a role which he could fulfil by becoming Bloom's son-in-law (570/695). But Bloom is also interested in Stephen as a friend, and it is here that the transsexual explorations of the novel focus. 'Love between man and man is impossible because there must not be sexual intercourse': Joyce first showed an interest in sexual feeling in male friendship when he copied this observation from Stanislaus's diary into 'A Painful Case' (*D*, 125). *Exiles*, written after Joyce had begun *Ulysses*, does not give up so easily. The notes for the play show Joyce's interest in triangular relationships which bring men surrogately into sexual contact. These relationships are not, as in the conventional form invoked in *Ulysses* by Eglinton (175/213), a ground of rivalry and aggression. As in the Shakespeare sonnets treated so prominently in Scylla and Charybdis, they are rather an extension of the possibilities of friendship and love. The *Exiles* notes explain:

> Bertha wishes for the spiritual union of Richard and Robert and *believes* (?) that union will be effected only through her body, and perpetuated thereby ... The bodily possession of Bertha by Robert, repeated often, would certainly bring into almost carnal contact the two men. Do they desire this? To be united, that is carnally through the person and body of Bertha as they cannot, without dissatisfaction and degradation, be united carnally man to man as man to woman? (*E*, 172)

This is very close to Joyce's somewhat less than obvious interpretation of a dream of Nora's of 1916: 'Prezioso weeping / I have passed him in the street / My book 'Dubliners' in his hand'. Joyce saw in this 'a secret disappointment that for her so far it is impossible to unite the friendship of two men' (himself and Prezioso) 'through the gift of herself differently to both' (*JJ*, 437). The amount of reading-in that this 'interpretation' requires suggests that the disappointment may not have been so simply Nora's. The possibility of surrogate sexual contact, explicit in the *Exiles* notes, is left implicit in the play: Richard feels that Robert's making love to Bertha draws the two men together (*E*,106); he finds it exciting to hear in physical detail how Robert makes love to his wife (*E*, 116–17); the 'motive deeper still' (*E*, 98) than those he can specify for positively wanting Robert to make love to Bertha is evidently that spelled out by the notes – a longing for surrogate sexual union with his friend. In one of the rejected fragments of dialogue for the play, Joyce implies that these feelings are not unusual when he identifies pain usually understood as jealousy as frustrated homosexual longing.[6] Joyce would have found it even more difficult than he did to get the play performed in 1917 if he had written any of this in explicitly. As it stands, the play was rejected as indecent by the Stage Society (*JJ*, 415, 443). But without the notes the homosexual theme was evident to an alert early commentator[7].

'Greater love than this ... no man hath that a man lay down his wife for his friend' (*U*, 322/393). When *Ulysses* is read in the light of *Exiles* Stephen's remark appears more than the witty blasphemy he intends. Beaumont and Fletcher, friends who share a lover (322/393),and in a more extended way the discussion of Shakespeare's sonnets, all prepare the ground for the sexual implications of Bloom's interest in Stephen. Bloom finds pleasure in the idea of Molly having sex with other men. Molly supposes that he made arrangements to facilitate her affair with Boylan. Clearly she is right to suspect that Bloom has plans for Stephen and herself as lovers.[8] Bloom's dwelling on Parnell and Kitty O'Shea has an undercurrent of Stephen and Boylan (his 'younger men' version of the scenario (535/656) does not fit the surface situation). He shows Stephen Molly's photo in a way designed to provoke sexual interest. Having Stephen as a lodger promises his 'vicarious satisfaction' (570/695). Stephen's dream too, which (as its pointed recall indicates (179/217) is a premonition of his meeting with Bloom, also previsions Bloom's offer of Molly. One strand of the dream-prophecy is fulfilled when Bloom becomes the man in the dream and its Haroun Al Raschid (466/571–2; 478/586). Since the man is Bloom, the melon he holds out to Stephen must be Molly, with whom the melon is so emphatically associated (604/734). The identification is reinforced by the dream's Middle-Eastern setting (325/397; 359/439). 'And why not?' is Bloom's attitude (534/654): why should Stephen and Molly not be lovers? He rejects the convention that scandal and secrecy should surround sexual relations outside marriage. To engineer for Stephen a relationship with Molly is a way of taking care of him (saving him from prostitutes and disease), and of driving out Boylan. But there is, as in *Exiles*, a motive deeper still.

As with *Exiles* this was evident to the best-informed of early commentators. Frank Budgen remarks Bloom's 'wish to share his wife with other men': 'that his wife is possessed by other males gives his physical contact with them at second hand"[9]. This is precisely the theme of the *Exiles* notes, then unpublished, but evidently Budgen would have been alerted to Joyce's interest in conversation. In *Ulysses* Joyce points to his theme, as usual, by implicatory detail. The significant episode is Eumaeus, the beginning of the Nostos, 'fusion of Bloom and Stephen' in the Linati schema. *The Merchant of Venice*, with its sexually charged emotional friendship between Antonio and Bassanio, is invoked in relation to the Antonio tattoo of pseudo-Ulysses Murphy (520/636). The tattoo's sixteen in European slang and in numerology signified homosexuality,[10] which may explain Murphy's enigmatic innuendo when questioned about the number: 'A Greek he was' ('Greeker than the Greeks' is Mulligan's way of identifying Bloom's supposed homosexuality). Bloom has both his act and his cases muddled, but the Criminal Law Amendment Act he has in mind is that used against Oscar Wilde (527–8/645–6). The 'Cornwall case' to which Bloom slithers associatively via Edward, Prince of Wales, Duke of Cornwall, was a homosexual scandal of 1883 involving two officials of Dublin Castle, Cornwall and French. Clearly 'jockeys and esthetes ... and other member of the upper ten' are not only adulterers. With sixteen and Antonio mixed into this medley, Joyce's variations on his theme seem almost insistent. Eumaeus ends with a typical symbolic touch: by entwining Bloom and Stephen with snatches of a wedding ballad the road sweeper presents them as lovers.

Bloom and Stephen have their mutually instigated pee together after Bloom has shared with Stephen his love for Molly. The moment is blessed by a celestial sign: a star passes from the Lyre of Orpheus (male, artist, Stephen), through the Coma Berenices (promise fulfilled to Aphrodite, symbol of love, female, Molly), to Leo. With the *Exiles*/transsexual/homosexual/ Eumaeus background in view it would be a severely literal reader who could see in this only a Swiftian excretory humour. Joyce infers the usually sublimated sexual element in male friendship without tipping this over into the fully homosexual feelings which would narrow his implications.

3

Comedy

One of Joyce's greatest gifts is for comedy, which for Joyce is both a view of the world (*commedia*), and an attitude to perception, fictional form and language. In his Paris notebook (1903) Joyce evolved a theory of comedy as 'the perfect manner in art', relating comic joy to the emotional stasis proper to all aesthetic pleasure (*CW*, 144). Comedy is, then, theoretically central to Joyce's work from the beginning, but in *Dubliners* only 'Grace' – indicatively on the adaptations and compromises of the 'Church diplomatic' (*SH*, 155) – is fully (and darkly) comic. In *A Portrait of the Artist* comedy is largely irony against Stephen: there is little laughter. In *Ulysses*, however, comedy is central, comprehensive in its targets – character, theme, medium; and in its types – mockery, satire, parody, black humour of emotional trauma and death, humour mingled with pathos, joyous laughter which draws on clowning, music-hall and other popular forms. Susanne Langer, a theorist of comedy who is ready to descend from the exaltation of seasonal cycle and fertility rite to consider laughter and jokes, sees comedy in a thoroughly Joycean way, as enhancing the vitality of life.[1] Langer presents her view in terms of the rhythms of comic drama, but the effect she describes can be derived equally from any artistic shaping that issues in affirmative laughter – what Jacques Derrida, in a teasingly comic account of Joycean comedy, hesitates to call (but nonetheless calls) Joyce's dominant effect: *oui-rire/yes in laughter*.[2] After all the specific points have been made about the location of Joyce's voices and the relation of

Joyce to Stephen and to Bloom, it is in the affirmation of this 'yes in laughter' that one overall meaning of *Ulysses* lies. It also provides one answer to Joyce's gloomier critics. The Bakhtinian notion of carnival offers one way of describing this Langer/Derrida sense of affirmative comedy more fully. Comedy can be normative: utilitarian laughter which restrains eccentricity, saturnalia which contains licence by providing a permitted and regulated outlet. Comedy can also be subversive: unassimilably nonofficial, forever escaping containment by the ordered and fixed. This is carnival as formulated by Bakhtin in his attempt to understand Rabelais by relating his work to mediaeval traditions of socially disruptive comedy.[3] In Bakhtin's account, a central mode of carnival is parody, relevant to Joyce not only in the linguistic parodies of Cyclops, Nausikaa and Oxen of the Sun but also in the relation of the whole novel to Homer. As in *Ulysses* so in Bakhtinian carnival the bodily functions of eating, excretion and sex are presented openly, and not as degrading but as elements of common humanity, parts of the cyclical processes of death and birth, which in the carnival context laughter acknowledges as regenerative. Like Rabelais, Joyce draws extensively on popular culture: the reader must be as ready to respond to the transformation of a music-hall song as to a metamorphosis of Homer. Above all, Bakhtin sees carnival's opposition to the completed and ordered world of the official as profoundly in tune with the perpetually uncompleted nature of being itself. In the eternally relative is the joy of change. It is in this refusal of closure that Bakhtin's conception of carnival is most relevant to *Ulysses*. The events of a single day are inevitably unresolved: how Bloom and Molly's relations will be affected by it, what role (if any) Stephen will play in their lives, we are left to suppose. And Joyce draws attention to purposely loose ends and gaps: 'Who was M'Intosh?'; what happened to Bloom in 'a blank period of time' between Cyclops and Nausikaa (599/729)? The variety of styles with no governing authorial voice, the clashes of perspective between which judgements are only implied, the often ambiguous symbolic writing, are aspects of form with a similar partial indeterminacy.

There is a comparable destabilising of individual identity in the continuous Homeric parallels, the transformations of Circe, the impostures of Eumaeus, and the play with names of Scylla and Charybdis (and elsewhere: Virag/Bloom/Flower; Jesus, Mr Doyle),[4] as there is in the duplication of parents in children ('Milly, Marionette' (366/448)), the identifications of Bloom and others (Sipold), and above all of Bloom and Stephen. And: 'that other world' (for 'word' (63/77)); throwaway/Throwaway; Bloo/Bloom/Blood (124/151); Boy/Boylan/du Boyes (528/647): verbal mistakes combine with Joyce's love of punning further to heighten indeterminacy by multiplying the reference of words. So too does the sub-punning matching (or wrenching) of vocabulary to theme which Joyce so wittily deploys throughout *Ulysses*. This can be most clearly seen in the more extravagant dislocations of *Finnegans Wake*: for example, the complex crescendo of transformed ecclesiastical and celestial hierarchies, liturgical colours, canonical hours, sacraments, and gifts of the Holy Spirit which imbue the exaltation to sainthood of 'poor Kevin' (605–6). And though it is not until the *sui generis* experiment of the *Wake* that Joyce continuously destabilises the relation of word and referent, there are parts of *Ulysses* which do this in effect. It is possible, for example, to locate and make sense of every utterance in the closing section of Oxen of the Sun, but for most readers the multiplicity of voices in Burke's is no less Babelish than the similar cacophony of competing speakers in HCE's pub (*FW*, II. 3). The gaiety of carnival at Burke's, perpetually escaping the containment of sober sense, though extreme is epitomic.

Opposite to this drunken jollity is Joyce's sometimes grim comedy of sexual trauma, racial persecution, or political and religious violence, which can have an effect as in Samuel Beckett: subjects are transformed by their treatment, but not utterly. In *Finnegans Wake* Shem is a 'tragic jester' (171), a Joycean combination echoed in the complementary brothers, Tristopher and Hilary.[5] The comedy of *Ulysses* includes painful, even potentially tragic material, and despite the prevailing comic tone keeps uncomfortably in view its consequences of real suffering.

Molly's adultery, though Bloom accepts it, is at times deeply painful to him. The deaths of Stephen's mother and of Bloom's son, Bloom's father's suicide, and his underlying knowledge of the possibility of racial persecution, are all more than painful. But as in Shakespeare, the recognition that comedy is a matter of emphasis not exclusion, that it is achieved not by turning away from but by subsuming what threatens it, strengthens the validity of the comic vision. In *Finnegans Wake* Joyce prays, 'Loud, heap miseries upon us yet entwine our arts with laughters low!'.[6] It is his constant response. In a central episode of the *Wake* he tells his father's story of how Buckley, an Irish soldier in the Crimean War, finds in his gun-sights a Russian general. As Buckley is about to shoot, the general lets down his breeches to defecate. Moved by the ordinary and vulnerable humanity of the situation Buckley does not pull the trigger. But the general wipes himself with a piece of turf and at that insult to Ireland Buckley shoots. As the company in HCE's pub enjoys the story Joyce presents their lives and laughters all tinged with foliage, though shadowed by the darkness of death:

> And they leaved the most leavely of leaftimes and the most folliagenous till there came the marrer of mirth and the jangtherapper of all jocolarinas and they were as were they never ere. Yet had they laughtered, one on other, undo the end and enjoyed their laughings merry was the times when so grant it High Hilarion us may too! (361)

Laughter is not evergreen, but jocoserious fictions undo the end: they are an antidote to the truly foolish 'wisdom' of taking mortality mournfully. This is the response of the tragic jester, and a principle of Joyce's art.

Not all jesting, though, makes for spiritual health. Joyce is as doubtful as Stephen of one of the jester's tones: mockery. Mocker Mulligan plays, as Stephen could (21/25), the role of jester, complete with motley and bauble (162/197). In the transformations of Circe this becomes his identity (473/580). He is genuinely funny. He jokes as well as anybody about religion, sex, Ireland, Stephen – all Joyce's own subjects. But, '*Was Du verlachst wirst Du noch dienen*' ('What you laugh at you will nevertheless serve' (162/197)). A proverb with several applications, of Mulligan this means that the rebellion expressed by his mockery is the mask of a conventional nature. His remarks on Stephen's mother ('beastly dead'), his D.B.C conversation with Haines about Stephen ('He can never be a poet' (204/249)), and the altercation with Stephen at Westland Row (506–7/619–20) show the violence and drive to betray which underlie his superficially attractive persona. Mockery is comedy's Scylla as tragedy is its Charybdis.

Comedy has one final value for Joyce. When Stephen laughs to free his mind from his mind's bondage (174/212) he indicates laughter's ethical and political function. The sense of comedy with which Bloom is so richly endowed, and the self-irony of which Stephen is capable, are forces against fanaticism. Certainly Joyce took himself seriously: that was one perspective. He also practised irony as the sign of a civilised attitude to conviction, as in his comic, painful, and fundamentally serious account of himself as the artist as anarchist (*Letters*, II, 206). Joyce therefore allows comedy to play over everything, including his various self-portraits and those areas of *Ulysses* which imply his own positive values: Bloom's political statements (Cyclops set against Eumaeus), Stephen's confrontation with church and state, Bloom's vision of Rudy inspired by contact with Stephen, Stephen and Bloom's moment of communion. None of this is satire. Joyce's comedy is often affectionate, just as his irony can be sympathetic. The fact of laughter is as important as the duality of vision. The serious is not solemn. Always more than a single perspective is possible. No-one in *Ulysses* is further from self-irony than the bigoted and hypocritical citizen. That is why he is Polyphemus: one-eyed, fanatical, he is the antitype of Joyce, for whom the perspective of laughter is a contribution to intellectual freedom.

*

Either the perception of a great truth, or the opening up of a great question, or a great conflict which is almost independent of the conflicting actors, and has been and is of far-reaching importance – this is what primarily rivets our attention. Ibsen has chosen the average lives in their uncompromising truth.   (CW, 63)

'A great truth ... a great question ... a great conflict ... average lives in their uncompromising truth'. The great seen in the average, as Joyce praised it in Ibsen, is central to *Ulysses*, which combines the ordinary of its precise location and fully depicted characters with the exceptional of myth. Bloom is impossible to sum up: the comprehensiveness of Odysseus was what appealed to Joyce. Keynotes are: family relationships, a qualified idealism, and a humorous scepticism which tests the received and is a ground both for intellectual and emotional adventure and acceptance of limitation. Stephen is a more typically modern hero, out of Goethe or Dostoievsky, but also with classic parallels, the artist and intellectual, alienated (Hamlet) and in revolt (Lucifer). In Stephen Joyce tests the Ibsenite theme of the duty of self-fulfilment, escaping the limits set by age and society, and examines the egotism of this stance which is itself a form of limitation. Individual and typical, Bloom and Stephen are in various ways related because, though antitypes, they are also complementary. *Ulysses* is about characters and about what constitutes consciousness and individual identity. It is also a portrait of the exterior working and consequences for individual feeling of a civilisation of which Joyce's scrupulous honesty gives a clear vision without either sentimentality of brutality. The novel is, too, encyclopaedic of the possibilities or English: what the language can express and depict, what this means about available modes of feeling, and what can be done with the language in terms of shape and music. It is the comprehensiveness of its social and historical scope, its characters and myths, its religious, sexual and political themes, its experiments with form and language, which make *Ulysses* amenable to so many different kinds of analysis. They also make it difficult to see whole.

Joyce endorsed some traditional interests of criticism. His experimental attitudes to form, language, gender and the nature and presentation of consciousness generated experimental modes of criticism which, in the hands of codifying proselytes, have sought to become the new orthodoxy by polemically caricaturing the kinds of criticism Joyce sanctioned. What Joyce accepted – even in some cases collaborated in producing – no reader of *Ulysses* does well to ignore, while the foolish and imaginary 'proofs' of the *Wake*'s Professor Jones – 'proved to mindself as to your sotisfiction' (161) – should be a warning to intellectuals who treat Joyce as grist for a favourite theory. Continual experiment is more in tune with Joyce's work than orthodoxies, old or new.

Appendix

THE SCHEMATA

In *Finnegans Wake* (119–23) Joyce draws a parallel between
that novel and the illuminations of *The Book of Kells*: their
elaborate detail encodes secret meanings within a firm structure
which permits an exuberant riot of invention. *Ulysses* is drawn
into this analogy. Joyce's schemata for the novel show why it
should be. There are two main schemata. The first was made
in September 1920 for Carlo Linati. The second, made in
November 1921 for Valéry Larbaud's Paris lecture on *Ulysses*
of December that year, was used by Stuart Gilbert in his *James
Joyce's 'Ulysses'*. (A third, sent to John Quinn in September
1920, outlines simply the Homeric subjects of the episodes and
the novel's three-fold division into Telemachia, Odyssey and
Nostos (*Letters*, I, 145).) The Linati schema, written in Italian,
was made just over a year before the novel was finished. Joyce
described the schema to Linati as 'per uso puramente domestico'
(for home use only). It is considerably more elaborate than the
later schema, containing one whole section not in Gilbert (Senso
[Significato]/Sense [Meaning]), a different kind of identification
of predominant symbols, more Homeric correspondences, and
many other differences of detail. Some of these suggest how
much the novel changed even in late stages of development:
others indicate how tentative some of the schematic elements
always were. There is a complete transcription and translation
of the Linati schema in Richard Ellmann's *Ulysses on the Liffey*.[1]

I TELEMACHIA

TITLE	SCENE	HOUR	ORGAN	ART	COLOUR
1. Telemachus	The Tower	8 a.m.		theology	white, gold
2. Nestor	The School	10 a.m.		history	brown
3. Proteus	The Strand	11 a.m.		philology	green

II ODYSSEY

TITLE	SCENE	HOUR	ORGAN	ART	COLOUR
1. Calypso	The House	8 a.m.	kidney	economics	orange
2. Lotus eaters	The Bath	10 a.m.	genitals	botany, chemistry	
3. Hades	The Graveyard	11 a.m.	heart	religion	white, black
4. Eolus	The Newspaper	12 noon	lungs	rhetoric	red
5. Lestrygonians	The Lunch	1 p.m.	esophagus	architecture	
6. Scylla and Charybdis	The Library	2 p.m.	brain	literature	
7. Wandering Rocks	The Streets	3 p.m.	blood	mechanics	
8. Sirens	The Concert Room	4 p.m.	ear	music	
9. Cyclops	The Tavern	5 p.m.	muscle	politics	
10. Nausikaa	The Rocks	8 p.m.	eye, nose	painting	grey, blue
11. Oxen of Sun	The Hospital	10 p.m.	womb	medecine	white
12. Circe	The Brothel	12 midnight	locomotor apparatus	magic	

III NOSTOS

TITLE	SCENE	HOUR	ORGAN	ART	COLOUR
1. Eumeus	The Shelter	1 a.m.	nerves	navigation	
2. Ithaca	The House	2 a.m.	skeleton	science	
3. Penelope	The Bed		flesh		

SYMBOL	TECHNIC	CORRESPONDENCES
heir	narrative (young)	Stephen – Telemachus, Hamlet: Buck Mulligan – Antinous: Milkwoman – Mentor.
horse	catechism (personal)	Deasy – Nestor: Pisistratus – Sargent: Helen – Mrs O'Shea.
tide	monologue (male)	Proteus – Primal Matter: Kevin Egan – Menelaus: Megapenthus – the Cocklepicker.
nymph	narrative (mature)	Calypso – the Nymph: Dlugacz – the Recall: Zion – Ithaca.
eucharist	narcissism	Lotuseaters – Cabhorses, Communicants, Soldiers, Eunuchs, Bather, Watchers of Cricket.
caretaker	incubism	Dodder, Grand and Royal Canals, Liffey – the 4 Rivers: Cunningham – Sisyphus: Father Coffey – Cerberus: Caretaker – Hades: Daniel O'Connell – Hercules: Dignam – Elpenor: Parnell – Agamemnon: Menton – Ajax.
editor	enthymemic	Crawford – Eolus: Incest – journalism: Floating Island – press.
constables	peristaltic	Antiphates – Hunger: The Decoy – Food: Lestrygonians – Teeth.
Stratford, London	dialectic	The Rock – Aristotle, Dogma, Stratford: The Whirlpool – Plato, Mysticism, London: Ulysses – Socrates, Jesus, Shakespeare.
Citizens	labyrinth	Bosphorus – Liffey: European Bank – Viceroy: Asiatic Bank – Conmee: Symplegades – groups of citizens.
barmaids	fuga per canonem	Sirens – barmaids: Isle – bar.
fenian	gigantism	Noman – I: Stake – cigar: challenge – apotheosis.
virgin	tumescence, detumescence	Phaeacia – Star of the Sea: Gerty – Nausikaa.
mothers	embryonic development	Hospital – Trinacria: Lampetie, Phaethusa – Nurses: Helios – Horne: Oxen – Fertility: Crime – Fraud.
whore	hallucination	Circe – Bella.
sailors	narrative (old)	Eumeus – Skin the Goat: Sailor – Ulysses Pseudoangelos: Melanthius – Corly.
comets	catechism (impersonal)	Eurymachus – Boylan: Suitors – scruples: Bow – Reason.
earth	monologue (female)	Penelope – Earth: Web – Movement.

The schema printed here is that made for Larbaud and used by Stuart Gilbert.[2] Unlike the Linati schema it was made from the start with a degree of public intention (for a lecture), and Joyce sanctioned its public use and partial publication in Stuart Gilbert's book. Nevertheless, in 1933 he declined to allow his American publisher, Random House, to issue the Gilbert schema with the novel (*Letters*, III, 291). The importance of the schemata has always been controversial. Pound dismissed them, for critical purposes: they were a help to Joyce; they are of no importance to the reader.[3] Certainly the importance of their different elements varies from section to section. Joyce's own attitude to them may have depended on their likely use. They could be used to defend the novel against charges of formlessness, but probably Joyce did not want to make the novel's structure, patterned detail, or Homeric relationships too prominent, in keeping with his doubt later expressed to Beckett: 'I may have oversystematized *Ulysses*' (*JJ*, 702).

Notes

PREFACE

1. This view of criticism is argued more fully, with some differences of emphasis, in my *Blake's Heroic Argument*, London, Croom Helm, 1987, Chapter 4, 'Discussing Literature and Writing Criticism'. I also describe there the experiences and values in politics, religion and sexuality operative in my view of Blake. Though my experience has recently shifted somewhat in both religion and sexuality – and in such a way that *Heroic Argument*'s essay on religion particularly now requires a positive complement – still, similar underlying values to those described there are operative in the view of *Ulysses* that follows.

HISTORICAL AND CULTURAL CONTEXT

1. Dominic Manganiello's excellent overall account, *Joyce's Politics*, London, Routledge, 1980, shows how much is to be gained by taking seriously Herbert Gorman's list of Joyce's reading in anarchist writers (in *James Joyce*, London, John Lane, 1941, 183).
2. *Letters*, II, 48, 148. cf. the satire of religious anti-socialist propaganda in *SH*, 133, 154–5, and Joyce to Arthur Power on the writer's function: to maintain a continual struggle against the norms imposed by the church and conventional patterns of social life (in *Conversations with James Joyce*, London, Millington, 1974, 74).
3. Stanislaus Joyce, *My Brother's Keeper*, London, Faber & Faber, 1958, 174.

4. Robert Scholes and R. M. Kain (eds), *The Workshop of Daedalus*, Evanston, Illinois University Press, 1965, 68.
5. Stanislaus Joyce (1958), *op. cit.*, 173.
6. In a short space it is impossible to give any full notion of Joyce's relation to his contemporaries. I have concentrated here on issues which give basic orientations in aesthetics, ethics and religion for the account of *Ulysses* which follows. Not all the relevant contexts are high-cultural. Since the reconstruction of Joyce's Trieste library by Richard Ellmann (*The Consciousness of Joyce*, London, Faber & Faber, 1977) several studies have examined Joyce's interaction with popular fiction and journalism. See especially Cheryl Herr, *Joyce's Anatomy of Culture*, Urbana, Illinois University Press, 1986, and R. B. Kershner, *Joyce, Bakhtin and Popular Literature*, Chapel Hill, University of North Carolina Press, 1989, though Kershner excludes *Ulysses* from specific consideration. Drawing on Foucault and Fredric Jameson in terms of method, Cheryl Herr shows how, in specific allusions and by the process of alluding, Joyce interacts with the ideological assumptions of his society as these are reflected in the press, music-hall and popular theatre, and sermons, and how Joyce subverts these institutional discourses by focusing on conflicts between ideologies. In addition, the significant literary backgrounds of Joyce's work are not all contemporary. Joyce enormously admired Ben Jonson, for example (see Frank Budgen, *James Joyce and the Making of 'Ulysses'*, London, Faber & Faber, 1934; reprinted, Oxford University Press, 1972, 186), whose work has much in common with his own: the combination of realism and comic fantasy, the definition of subjects by accretion of detail in Jonson's plays, the formal elegance and purity of diction of his poetry. Aristotle and Dante were both important influences: Stephen's mind is full of Aristotelian concepts; Joyce's loss of faith in the premises of the universal explanation the *Commedia* embodies did not mean a loss of admiration for its intellectual and imaginative power. The combined influence of materialist philosopher and religious visionary is indicatively paradoxical: Joyce chose Defoe and Blake for his Trieste lectures to illustrate 'realism and idealism in English Literature' (*CW*, 214) because his work has elements in common with both writers. But the materialist/visionary combination is already there in Dante himself. Aristotle filtered through Aquinas is central to the *Commedia*: though Aristotle's shade is in Limbo, his ideas structure the poem's universe. The encyclopaedic *Commedia*, with its variety of styles, portrait of the artist as a younger man, and eclectic cultural scope, is as much analogous to *Ulysses* as the more direct Homeric model.

7. Frank Budgen ([1934], 1972), *op. cit.*, 20.

8. 'Nothing in *Madame Bovary* is true ... I put into it nothing of my own feelings nor of my own life'; 'I am Madame Bovary', *CW*, 141. *Madame Bovary*, Edouard Maynial (ed.), Paris, éditions Garnier, 1961, xxi.

9. As in Hugh Kenner, *Dublin's Joyce*, Bloomington, Indiana University Press, 1956; reprinted, New York, Columbia University Press, 1987, I. 6.

10. Herbert Gorman (1941), *op cit.*, 226–7.

11. 'Mr Bennett and Mrs Brown' and 'Modern Fiction', in Virginia Woolf, *Collected Essays*, London, Chatto & Windus, 4 vols, 1966, Vol. I, 319–37, Vol. II, 103–10.

12. The metaphor of the stream of thought or consciousness was coined at the turn of the century by the philosopher and psychologist, William James. The idea of *monologue intérieur* Joyce liked to say had come to him from the novelist Eduard Dujardin (*JJ*, 126). There have been several attempts to establish distinctions in the use of these two terms (see, for example, Erwin R. Steinberg, *The Stream-of-Consciousness Technique in the Modern Novel*, New York, Kennikat Press, 1979, esp. 144–63), but the distinctions have not gained general currency.

13. *JJ*, 661; Ezra Pound, *Selected Letters*, D. D. Paige (ed.), London, Faber & Faber, 1950, 202.

14. Frank Budgen ([1934], 1972), *op. cit.*, 191; *P*, 248.

15. *Letters*, II, 90, 91. Blake is several times referred to in *Ulysses* as part of the characterisation of Stephen's outlook as heterodox. Shelley is a presence throughout Joyce's work, particularly two crucial passages from *A Defence of Poetry*, on the nature of poetic inspiration ('the mind in creation is as a fading coal': *CW*, 78, 182; *P*, 217; *U*, 160/197), and on the function of poets ('unacknowledged legislators') which Joyce echoes not verbally but substantially in *CW* (82), *SH* (75), and *P* (257). It is a line of thought in keeping with Joyce's sense of the oblique moral function of art.

16. 'Epiphany and the Epiphanies', in Zack Bowen and J. F. Carens (eds), *A Companion to Joyce Studies*, Westport and London, Greenwood, 1984, 707–25 (710).

CRITICAL RECEPTION: THEORETICAL PERSPECTIVES

1. See, for example, *Letters*, I, 175, and Frank Budgen ([1934], 1972), *op. cit.*, 194.

2. cf. *Letters*, I, 257 on the related viewpoint of the *Wake*, I, vi, 11.

3. Stuart Gilbert, *James Joyce's 'Ulysses'*, London, Faber & Faber, 1930; revised edn, 1952, 8–9; Frank Budgen ([1934], 1972), *op. cit.*, 17, 106–7.

4. Hugh Kenner's view of *Ulysses* is discussed further in II. For other critiques see the essays by Leslie Fiedler, 'Joyce and Jewish Consciousness', *Scripsi*, 2.1, 21–6, and William Empson, '*Ulysses*: Joyce's Intentions' and 'The Ultimate Novel', in *Using Biography*, London, Chatto & Windus, 1984.

5. Derrida's pieces on Joyce are printed in Derek Attridge and Daniel Ferrer (eds), *Post-structuralist Joyce*, Cambridge, Cambridge University Press, 1984 and Bernard Benstock (ed.), *James Joyce: The augmented ninth*, New York, Syracuse University Press, 1988. The first is concerned with the presence of Joyce in Derrida's earlier work, and with *Finnegans Wake*. The second is full of Derridean play with language, but has also a teasing narrative: personal circumstances of a *Ulyssean* kind give rise to reflections on expertise in criticism. Does this consist in mastering the scholarship, or having relevant experiences? Is not the notion of competence apparently held out by a James Joyce Foundation (which Derrida is addressing, stressing his own incompetence) radically impossible? In Kristeva's work Joyce is frequently source or example. Her most extended discussion (printed in Bernard Benstock, 1988, above) is an essay on imaginative identification through literature and love (*eros* and *agape*) replacing the identification with God once symbolised by the Eucharist. The 'carnivalized liturgy' of Joyce's language and the comprehensiveness of the quasi-mythic characters open the reader to this. Lacan's lectures and seminars on Joyce (Jacques Aubert (ed.), *Joyce avec Lacan*, Paris, Navarin Éditeur, 1987) have not been translated. Attracted to Joyce mainly by his verbal play, Lacan celebrates Joyce's work as ending the essentialist dream of finding meaning. More general consequences of Lacanian psychoanalysis for reading Joyce are discussed by various contributors to Benstock, including a dissident, Geert Lernout, who emerges like a being from intellectual pre-history to raise questions of logic, argument and evidence.

6. Roland Barthes, 'The Death of the Author', 1968, in *Image-Music-Text*, translated by Stephen Heath, London, Fontana, 1977, 142–9; Michel Foucault, 'What is an Author', 1969, translated by Josué V. Harari, in J. V. Harari (ed.), *Textual Strategies: Perspectives in post-structuralist criticism*, London, Methuen, 1979, 141–60.

7. *Letters*, II, 166; Frank Budgen ([1934], 1972), *op. cit.*, 69.

8. 'The Author's Many Voices', in Wayne Booth, *The Rhetoric of Fiction*, Chicago, Chicago University Press, 1961, 20.

9. See Bakhtin's discussion of Pushkin's *Evgenij Onegin* in *The Dialogic Imagination: Four essays*, translated by Caryl Emerson and Michael Holquist, Austin, Texas University Press, 1981. On Joyce and the dialogic see David Lodge, 'Joyce and Bakhtin: *Ulysses* and the typology of literary discourse', *The Journal of English Language and Literature* (Korea), 29, 121–30. (Bakhtin may have known Joyce's work, as other members of his circle certainly did, but found it impossible to mention in terms acceptable to the then prevailing Soviet orthodoxies. See R. B. Kershner (1989), *op. cit.*, 17).

10. See Phillip F. Herring, *Joyce's 'Ulysses' Notesheets in the British Museum*, Charlottesville, University of Virginia Press, 1972. For example, see Cyclops, 10, 41–3, and see Herring's commentary, 16–17.

1. THEMES AND TECHNIQUES

1. These protean transformations can be explained in terms that save the god from being eaten: see Don Gifford, *'Ulysses' Annotated*, Berkeley, University of California Press, 1988, 65.

2. Frank Budgen ([1934], 1972), *op. cit.*, 52.

3. Joyce questioned this Coleridgean view of Bruno in an early essay (CW, 134), but, with the reservations of usual *Wake* humour, apparently accepted it later (*FW*, 92).

4. 8,248/9; 50,218/61. (Differences in both places in editions before Gabler make the connecting repetitions here less precise). There are many other echoes. Both think about such miscellaneous subjects as Turko the Terrible (9/10; 47/57), Palestrina (17/21; 67/82), navelcords (32/38; 92/112), the Fenian leader, James Stephens (36/43, 'the head centre'; 56/68), and the Sandycove drowning. Both derive humour from aspects of Christ's Passion (42/50; 71/86). Bloom even has his own version of Stephen's poem (40,398/48; 55,450/67).

5. This is again an issue on which Bloom's and Stephen's views coincide: cf. Stephen on the corpsechewer God and *dio boia* (9/10, 175/213, 342/420, 474/581).

6. Since this demonstration is in part pro-Boer this is another detail that unites Bloom with Stephen (cf. 154, 133–8/187).

7. Bloom is more aware of Lenehan and others than they suppose (304,891–3/371, and cf. 192–3/234).

8. Behind Stephen's thought is a novel Joyce reviewed in 1903. See *CW*, 118.

9. Richard Ellmann (ed.), *Giacomo Joyce*, London, Faber & Faber, 1968, xxi.

10. *JJ*, 448–53; *Letters*, II, 426–36.

11. See *Letters*, II, 242, and epiphanies 7 and 34, in Robert Scholes and R. M. Kain (eds), *The Workshop of Daedalus*, Evanston, Illinois University Press, 1965, 17 and 44. cf. *SH*, 103 and 108. Stephen's vision of *A Portrait*, 4, is comparable to Nausikaa. Stephen 'worships' the girl; she is associated with the Virgin by the Virgin's traditional colours, her blue dress and ivory skin.

12. That Joyce took some trouble, however, with the stages of embryo development is evident from his notes for this episode. See Phillip F. Herring (1972), *op. cit.*, 164–5, and illustration between 162 and 163.

13. Stanley Sultan, *The Argument of 'Ulysses'*, Columbus, Ohio State University Press, 1964, 282–6.

14. After the opening invocations the styles parodied are Latin translation (314/383 [meaning disappears beneath ornate grammar]), Anglo-Saxon (315/384 [rhythmic, alliterative]), generalised Middle English (316/386), Mandeville (316/386), Malory (317/387), Elizabethan chronicle (320/391), various early seventeenth-century styles (321/392 [including the Authorised Version and Sir Thomas Browne]), Bunyan (323/395), seventeenth-century diarists (324/396), Defoe (326/398), Swift (327/399 [manner of *A Tale of a Tub*]), eighteenth-century essayists (328/401 [Addison and Steele]), Sterne (330/404 [manner of *A Sentimental Journey*]), Goldsmith (332/406), Burke (333/407), various late eighteenth-century styles (333/408 [including Sheridan (political writings) and perhaps Samuel Johnson]), Junius (334/409), Gibbon (335/410), Gothic novel (336/412), Lamb (337/412 [childhood sentiment]), De Quincey (338/414 [opium dream]), Landor (338/415 [*Imaginary Conversations* in classical settings]), Macaulay (340/416 [history improved]), T. H. Huxley (341/418 [cheerful faith in scientific rationalism]), Dickens (343/420 [particularly *David Copperfield*]), Newman (344/421), Pater (344/422), Ruskin (344/422), Carlyle (344/423), modern miscellany – dialect, slang, hot gospeller, etc. (346/424). Joyce composed Oxen not simply from his own reading but from two text books, Saintsbury's *History of English Prose Rhythm* and Peacock's anthology, *English Prose: Mandeville to Ruskin*.

15. D. H. Lawrence, *The Complete Letters*, Harry T. Moore (ed.), 2 vols, London, Heinemann, 1962, 1087 (cf. 1075, 76).

16. Harry Levin, *James Joyce*, 1941, 105–6.

17. Bloom's main fantasies are of his trial (370–87/453–75); of being

acclaimed and martyred (390–407/478–99); of his grandfather, Virag (417–26/511–23, with brothel interruptions); of changing sex; of dialogue with the *Photo–Bits* Nymph (430–52/528–54); and of Molly and Boylan having sex (460–63/563–7).

18. 439,3057/538; 'rerere' is stammering horror, but 'rere' is also Joyce's usual archaic spelling for 'rear'.
19. 386/473; cf. 85/103, 281/343.
20. Hugh Kenner, *Dublin's Joyce*, Bloomington, Indiana University Press, 1956; reprinted, New York, Columbia University Press, 1987, 218.
21. 156/189; cf. 10,311–12/11; 35,182/41.
22. 474,4214–15/581 repeats 140,726/171; 473,4182/580 repeats 84,546/102.
23. 'The simple fact of the case was it was simply a case of ... '; cf. ll, 219, 820, 1103, 1114, 1308, 1533–4, 1590–1, 1647, 1682, 1872. For the drifting sentences see 515/630, 524–5/641–2, 527–8/645–6.
24. 'The only bond that is established between Bloom and Stephen is utterly commercial and utterly imaginary', Gerald Bruns, in Clive Hart and David Hayman (eds), *James Joyce's 'Ulysses': Critical essays*, Berkeley, University of California Press, 1974, 383.
25. Stuart Gilbert ([1930], 1952), *op. cit.*, 370; Frank Budgen ([1934], 1972), *op. cit.*, 264.
26. See, for example, Kenner on Bloom as a parody of the Enlightenment; Hugh Kenner ([1956], 1987), *op. cit.*, 217.
27. Frank Budgen ([1934], 1972), *op. cit.*, 262–3. Perhaps because of his unease here Joyce worked into Ithaca an unusual number of specific references to the *Odyssey*, including: Odysseus hit by a thrown stool (579/705); Odysseus fumigating the house (580–81/707); the suitors' gifts to Penelope (600/730); Odysseus kissing the earth on his return (640/734–5); the ten year absence (605/736). Echoes ⌐ his kind are not, like the more fundamental parallels, thematic; recognising them can, however, affect the reader's sense of Joyce's tone.
28. This argument, presented in different ways by R. M. Adams, *Surface and Symbol: the consistency of James Joyce's 'Ulysses'*, Oxford, Oxford University Press, 1962, 35–43, and Stanley Sultan, (1964), *op. cit.*, 415–50, is now generally treated as fact: see, for example, Hugh Kenner ([1956], 1987), *op. cit.*, revised edn, xii–xiii.
29. 616,389–93/749. 'Stand' here means 'get an erection' (see *OED*, 'stand', 6c). The lieutenant was not literally falling over: he was not able to concentrate on sex because he was afraid 'wed be seen from the road'. Molly then contrasts this incapacity with her own state: 'and I so hot as I never felt'.

2. 'EXTRAVAGANT EXCURSIONS INTO FORBIDDEN TERRITORY' (*JJ*, 437)

Bloom, Stephen and the Joycean Triangle

1. The homosexual feeling implicit in Molly's relation with Hester Stanhope is explicit in the girlhood friendship of the *Exiles* notes (*U*, 622/756; *E*, 171). Within an aura of feeling which is implicitly sexual, Cranly proposes to Stephen a relation that goes beyond friendship (*P*, 251). Stephen twice recalls this in *Ulysses* with Mulligan (6/7, 41 [recall in Gabler edn only]). By invoking Wilde he identifies the feeling as homosexual.

2. Sigmund Freud, *Three Essays on the Theory of Sexuality*, 1905, in *Complete Psychological Works*, Standard Edition, James Strachey *et al.* (eds), London, Hogarth Press, 1953–74, 24 vols, Vol. vii, 145.

3. Phillip. F. Herring (1972), *op. cit.*, 252.

4. Obscene/episcene; soldiers/genitals (*FW*, 523).

5. *U*, 402–3/493–4. 'Latent ambidexterity' has probably the same meaning, though Partridge dates the use of 'ambidextrous' for bisexual only from *c.* 1935 (Eric Partridge, *Dictionary of Slang and Unconventional English*, 8th edn, Paul Beale (ed.), London, Routledge & Kegan Paul, 1984, 17).

6. John MacNicholas, *James Joyce's 'Exiles': A textual companion*, New York, Garland, 1979, Fragment III, 170.

7. See Samuel Tannenbaum in the 1919 *Little Review* symposium, in Robert Deming, *James Joyce: The critical heritage*, London, Routledge & Kegan Paul, 1970, 150–2.

8. Bloom finds pleasure (438/537); Molly supposes (630/766, 636/773); Molly suspects (637/774). And Stephen is hoping for the Shakespeare experience of being seduced by an older woman (157/191): it could make a writer of him. William Empson, 1984, *op. cit.*, 230–41, discusses Bloom's plans for Molly and Stephen acutely, but Empson undermines his arguments by insisting on their relation to suppositious Joyce biography and to knowing an implied end to *Ulysses* itself (Stephen returns and becomes Molly's lover, so enabling Bloom and Molly to resume sexual relations and have a son).

9. Frank Budgen ([1934], 1972), *op. cit.*, 149.

10. Don Gifford (1988), *op. cit.*, 544.

3. COMEDY

1. Susanne Langer, *Feeling and Form*, London, Routledge & Kegan NPaul, 1953, 345–50.
2. 'Ulysses Gramophone' in Bernard Benstock (1988) *op. cit.*, 57.
3. Mikhail Bakhtin, *Rabelais and his World*, translated by Helene Iswolsky, Cambridge, MA, MIT Press, 1968.
4. 509/622. See Don Gifford (1988), *op. cit.*, 539.
5. *FW*, 21; *tristis* (L.), sad; *hilarius* (L.), cheerful. cf. the hilariohoot and tristione of another equal and opposite pair, PW/WP (*FW*, 92).
6. *FW*, 259. 'Lord, have mercy upon us, and incline our hearts to keep this law': from the Communion service of the *Book of Common Prayer*.

APPENDIX: THE SCHEMATA

1. It is important to use the second corrected edition of *Ulysses on the Liffey* (1984) because Ellmann made mistakes in transcription and so in translation which were not fully corrected before this edition. The originals of the Linati and Gilbert schemata are reproduced in *The James Joyce Archive*, New York, Garland, 1977–79, Volume 12, '*Ulysses*', *Manuscripts & typescripts*, between 174 and 175.
2. It is transcribed with small emendations of punctuation to make clearer the connecting correspondences.
3. Ezra Pound, *Literary Essays of Ezra Pound*, T. S. Eliot (ed.), London, Faber & Faber, 1954, 406.

Select Bibliography

Abbreviations used in the text are indicated in brackets.

WORKS BY JAMES JOYCE

Collected Poems, New York, Viking Press, 1957.

Critical Writings, edited by Ellsworth Mason and Richard Ellmann, London, Faber & Faber, 1959. (*CW*)

Dubliners, edited by Robert Scholes in consultation with Richard Ellmann, London, Jonathan Cape, 1967. (*D*)

Exiles, with Joyce's own notes, introduction by Padraic Colum, London, Jonathan Cape, 1952. (*E*)

Finnegans Wake, London, Faber & Faber, 1939. (*FW*)

Giacomo Joyce, edited by Richard Ellmann, London, Faber & Faber, 1968.

Letters of James Joyce, 3 vols. Vol. I, edited by Stuart Gilbert, London, Faber & Faber, 1957; reissued with corrections, 1966. Vols II and III, edited by Richard Ellmann, London, Faber & Faber, 1966. (*Letters*, I, II and III)

Poems and Shorter Writings (including *Epiphanies*, *Giacomo Joyce* and 'A Portrait of the Artist'), edited by Richard Ellmann, A. Walton Litz and John Whittier–Ferguson, London, Faber & Faber, 1991.

A Portrait of the Artist as a Young Man, edited by Richard Ellmann, London, Jonathan Cape, 1968. The definitive text corrected from the Dublin holograph by Chester G. Anderson. (*P*)

Stephen Hero, edited by Theodore Spencer, revised by John J. Slocum and Herbert Cahoon, London, Jonathan Cape, 1956. (*SH*)

Selected Letters of James Joyce, edited by Richard Ellmann, London, Faber & Faber, 1975. (*SL*)

Ulysses, New York, Random House, 1961.

Ulysses, the corrected text edited by Hans Walter Gabler with Wolfhard Steppe and Claus Melchior, 3 vols, New York & London, Garland, 1984; without textual apparatus, in a single volume, Harmondsworth, Penguin, 1986; the 'Student's Edition' is the same text with lineated episodes. (*U*)

114

MANUSCRIPT MATERIALS

The James Joyce Archive, general editor Michael Groden, 63 vols, New York, Garland 1977–79 (a facsimile edition of all Joyce's extant notes, manuscripts, typescripts and corrected proofs).

MacNicholas, John, *James Joyce's 'Exiles': A textual companion*, New York, Garland, 1979 (contains rejected speeches).

Scholes, Robert and Kain, R. M. (eds.), *The Workshop of Daedalus*, Evanston, University of Illinois Press, 1965 (contains the complete epiphanies, the essay 'A Portrait of the Artist', and notebook materials).

BIOGRAPHICAL WORKS

Ellmann, Richard, *James Joyce*, Oxford, Oxford University Press, 1959; revised edn, 1982. (*JJ*)

Gorman, Herbert, *James Joyce*, London, John Lane, 1941.

Joyce, Stanislaus, *My Brother's Keeper: James Joyce's early years*, edited by Richard Ellmann, preface by T. S. Eliot, London, Faber & Faber, 1958.

Joyce, Stanislaus, *The Dublin Diary of Stanislaus Joyce*, edited by G. H. Healey, London, Faber & Faber, 1962; revised edn, *The Complete Dublin Diary of Stanislaus Joyce*, Ithaca, NY, Cornell University Press, 1971.

Mikhail, E. H., *James Joyce: Interviews and recollections*, London, Macmillan, 1990.

Power, Arthur, *Conversations with James Joyce*, edited by Clive Hart, London, Millington, 1974.

CRITICAL WORKS

Inevitably selective, the following list is an attempt to represent a full range of the approaches that *Ulysses* and Joyce's work more generally have attracted.

General

Attridge, Derek, *The Cambridge Companion to James Joyce*, Cambridge, Cambridge University Press, 1990.

Attridge, Derek and Ferrer, Daniel (eds.), *Post-structuralist Joyce*, Cambridge, Cambridge University Press, 1984.

Aubert, Jacques (ed.), *Joyce avec Lacan*, Paris, Navarin Éditeur, 1987.

Benstock, Bernard (ed.), *Critical Essays on James Joyce*, Boston, MA, Hall, 1985.

Benstock, Bernard (ed.), *James Joyce: The augmented ninth*, New York, Syracuse University Press, 1988.

Bowen, Zack and Carens, James F. (eds.), *A Companion to Joyce Studies*, Westport and London, Greenwood, 1984.

Boyle, Robert, S. J., *James Joyce's Pauline Vision: A Catholic exposition*, Carbondale, Southern Illinois University Press, 1978.

Brown, Richard, *James Joyce and Sexuality*, Cambridge, Cambridge University Press, 1985.

Cixous, Hélène, *The Exile of James Joyce*, translated by Sally A. J. Purcell, London, John Calder, 1976.

Deming, Robert, *James Joyce: The critical heritage*, 2 vols, London, Routledge & Kegan Paul, 1970.

Eco, Umberto, *The Aesthetics of Chaosmos: The middle ages of James Joyce*, translated by Ellen Esrock, Cambridge, MA, Harvard University Press, 1989.

Ellmann, Richard, *The Consciousness of Joyce*, London, Faber & Faber, 1977.

French, Marilyn, *The Book as World: James Joyce's 'Ulysses'*, Cambridge, MA, Harvard University Press, 1976.

Givens, Seon (ed.), *James Joyce: Two decades of criticism*, revised edn, New York, Vanguard, 1963.

Goldberg, S. L., *The Classical Temper*, London, Chatto & Windus, 1961.

Goldman, Arnold, *The Joyce Paradox*, London, Routledge & Kegan Paul, 1966.

Gross, John, *James Joyce*, London, Fontana, 1971.

Herr, Cheryl, *Joyce's Anatomy of Culture*, Urbana, University of Illinois Press, 1986.

Kenner, Hugh, *Dublin's Joyce*, Bloomington, IN, Indiana University Press, 1956; reprinted with a new preface, New York, NY, Columbia University Press, 1987.

Kenner, Hugh, *Joyce's Voices*, London, Faber & Faber, 1978.

Kershner, R. B., *Joyce, Bakhtin and Popular Literature*, Chapel Hill, University of North Carolina press, 1989.

Leavis, F. R., 'James Joyce and the Revolution of the Word', *Scrutiny*, II (1933), 193–201.

Levin, Harry, *James Joyce: A critical introduction*, London, Faber & Faber, 1941; revised edn, Norfolk, CT, New Directions, 1960.

Lewis, Wyndham, *Time and Western Man*, Chatto & Windus, 1927.

Litz, A. Walton, *The Art of James Joyce: Method and design in 'Ulysses' and 'Finnegans Wake'*, Oxford, Oxford University Press, 1961.

Litz, A. Walton, *James Joyce* (Twayne Authors Series), Boston, MA, Hall, 1964.

McCabe, Colin, *James Joyce and the Revolution of the Word*, London, Macmillan, 1978.

Manganiello, Dominic, *Joyce's Politics*, London, Routledge & Kegan Paul, 1980.

Mason, Ellsworth, 'James Joyce: Moralist', *Twentieth Century Literature*, I (1956), 196–206.

Morse, J. Mitchell, *The Sympathetic Alien: James Joyce and Catholicism*, London, Peter Owen, 1959.

Parrinder, Patrick, *James Joyce*, Cambridge, Cambridge University Press, 1984.

Peake, C. H., *James Joyce: The citizen and the artist*, Stanford, CA, Stanford University Press, 1977.

Riquelme, John Paul, *Teller and Tale in Joyce's Fiction: Oscillating perspectives*, Baltimore, MD, Johns Hopkins University Press, 1983.

Scott, Bonnie Kime, *Joyce and Feminism*, Brighton, Harvester, 1984.

Scott, Bonnie Kime, *James Joyce*, Brighton, Harvester, 1987.

Senn, Fritz, *Joyce's Dislocutions*, edited by J. P. Riquelme, Baltimore, MD, Johns Hopkins University Press, 1984.

Sullivan, Kevin, *Joyce Among the Jesuits*, New York, Columbia University Press, 1957.

Wilson, Edmund, 'James Joyce', *Axel's Castle*, New York, Scribners, 1931.

On 'Ulysses'

Adams, R. M., *Surface and Symbol: The consistency of James Joyce's 'Ulysses'*, Oxford, Oxford University Press, 1962.

Allott, Miriam, 'James Joyce: The Hedgehog and the Fox', Benedikz, B. S. (ed.), *On the Novel*, London, Dent, 1971, 161–77.

Blamires, Harry, *The Bloomsday Book*, London, Methuen, 1966; revised edn, *The New Bloomsday Book*, London, Routledge, 1988.

Budgen, Frank, *James Joyce and the Making of 'Ulysses'*, London, Faber & Faber, 1934; reprinted with other writings on Joyce, introduction by Clive Hart, Oxford, Oxford University Press, 1972.

Eliot, T. S., '*Ulysses*, Order and Myth', *The Dial*, November, 1923, 480–3 (reprinted in *Selected Prose of T. S. Eliot*, edited by Frank Kermode, London, Faber & Faber, 1975, 175–8).

Ellmann, Richard, *Ulysses on the Liffey*, London, Faber & Faber, 1972; with corrections, 1974; with further corrections, 1984.

Empson, William, '*Ulysses*: Joyce's intentions' and 'The Ultimate Novel', in Empson, William, *Using Biography*, London, Chatto & Windus, 1984, 203–16, 217–59.

Fiedler, Leslie, 'Bloom on Joyce: Or, Jokey for Jacob', *A Journal of Modern Literature*, I (1970), 19–29.

Fiedler, Leslie, 'Joyce and Jewish Consciousness', *Scripsi*, 2, 1, (1982), 21–6.

Gifford, Don with Seidman, Robert J., '*Ulysses*' Annotated, Berkeley, CA, University of California Press, 1988 (revised and enlarged edn of *Notes for Joyce: An annotation of James Joyce's 'Ulysses'*, New York, Dutton, 1974).

Gilbert, Stuart, *James Joyce's 'Ulysses'*, London, Faber & Faber, 1930; revised edn, 1952.

Hart, Clive, *James Joyce's 'Ulysses'*, Sydney, Sydney University Press, 1968.

Hart, Clive and Hayman, David (eds.), *James Joyce's 'Ulysses': Critical essays*, Berkeley, CA, University of California Press, 1974.

Hayman, David, '*Ulysses*': The mechanics of meaning, Madison, Wisconsin University Press, revised edn, 1982.

Hayman, David, 'Forms of Folly in Joyce: A study of clowning in *Ulysses*', *English Literary History*, 34 (1967), 260–83.

Herring, Phillip F., *Joyce's 'Ulysses' Notesheets in the British Museum*, Charlottesville, VA, University Press of Virginia, 1972.

Iser, Wolfgang, *The Implied Reader*, Baltimore, Johns Hopkins University Press, 1972 (chapters 7 and 8).

Jacquet, Claude, 'Les Plans de Joyce pour *Ulysses*', in Bonnerot, Louis (ed.), '*Ulysses*: cinquante ans après', Paris, Didier, 1974, 45–82.

Kain, Richard M., *Fabulous Voyager: James Joyce's 'Ulysses'*, Chicago, IL, Chicago University Press, 1947.

Kenner, Hugh, '*Ulysses*', London, Allen & Unwin, 1980; revised edn, Baltimore, MD, Johns Hopkins University Press, 1987.

Kettle, Arnold, '*Ulysses*', in Kettle, Arnold, *The English Novel: An introduction*, 2 vols, London, Hutchinson, 1961, vol. 2, 121–35.

Lawrence, Karen, *The Odyssey of Style in 'Ulysses'*, Princeton, NJ, Princeton University Press, 1981.

Litz, A. Walton, 'The Genre of *Ulysses*', in Halperin, John (ed.), *The Theory of the Novel*, Oxford, Oxford University Press, 1974, 109–20.

Lodge, David, 'Joyce and Bakhtin: *Ulysses* and the typology of literary discourse', *The Journal of English Language and Literature*, Korea, 29 (1983), 121–30.

Pound, Ezra, 'James Joyce and Pécuchet', translated by Fred Bornhauser, *Shenandoah*, III, 3 (1952), 9–20 (first published in French, *Mercure de France*, 1922. The French is reprinted, with all Pound's writings on Joyce, in *Pound / Joyce*, edited by Forrest Read, London, Faber & Faber, 1968).

Rabaté, Jean-Michel, *Joyce upon the Void: The genesis of doubt*, London, Macmillan, 1991.

Rabaté, Jean-Michel, *James Joyce, Unauthorized Reader*, Baltimore, MD, Johns Hopkins University Press, 1991.

Steinberg, Erwin R., *The Stream of Consciousness and Beyond in 'Ulysses'*, Pittsburgh, Pittsburgh University Press, 1973.

Sultan, Stanley, *The Argument of 'Ulysses'*, Columbus, Ohio State University Press, 1964.

Thomas, Brook, *James Joyce's 'Ulysses': A book of many happy returns*, Baton Rouge, Louisiana State University Press, 1982.

Thornton, Weldon, *Allusions in 'Ulysses'*, Chapel Hill, University of North Carolina Press, 1968.

CONTEXTS

Beckett, J. C., *A Short History of Ireland*, 3rd edn, London, Hutchinson, 1966.

Bradbury, Malcolm and McFarlane, James (eds.), *Modernism*, Harmondsworth, Penguin Books, 1976.

Deane, Seamus, *A Short History of Irish Literature*, London, Hutchinson, 1986.

Kain, R. M., *Dublin in the Age of William Butler Yeats and James Joyce*, Norman, Oklahoma University Press, 1962.

Kee, Robert, *The Green Flag*, London, Weidenfeld and Nicolson, 1972 (republished in 3 vols: *The Most Distressful Country*, *The Bold Fenian Men*, and *Ourselves Alone*, Harmondsworth, Penguin Books, 1989).

Kenner, Hugh, *The Pound Era*, London, Faber & Faber, 1971.

Shaw, G. B., *The Matter with Ireland*, London, Hart-Davies, 1962.

Stanford, W. B., *The Ulysses Theme*, Oxford, Blackwell, 1954.

Watson, G. J. B., *Irish Identity and the Literary Revival*, London, Croom Helm, 1979.

BIBLIOGRAPHICAL WORKS

Deming, Robert, *A Bibliography of James Joyce Studies*, 2nd edn, revised and enlarged, Boston, MA, Hall, 1977.

Finneran, Richard (ed.), *Anglo-Irish Literature: A review of research*, New York, Modern Language Association of America, 1976.

Finneran, Richard (ed.), *Recent Research on Anglo-Irish Writers*, New York, Modern Language Association of America, 1983.

Slocum, John and Cahoon, Herbert, *A Bibliography of James Joyce*, New Haven, CT, Yale University Press, 1953.

Staley, Thomas, *An Annotated Critical Bibliography of James Joyce*, Hemel Hempstead, Harvester Wheatsheaf, 1989.

James Joyce Quarterly, Oklahoma, University of Tulsa (publishes essays, reviews and a regular checklist of publications on Joyce.)

Index